ENDORSEMENTS

We often want to know the behind-the-scenes to some of our favorite events and the lives of some of our favorite people. That is exactly what *Dare to Be* offers, but it also gives more. After reading this book, you will walk away inspired, challenged, and ready to do the thing you've been wanting to do. It's a page-after-page reminder that God is faithful.

ANNIE F. DOWNS, *New York Times* bestselling author of *That Sounds Fun*

This book is such a beautiful overflow of what God has done in Charlotte's and Natalie's lives. I have no doubt it's going to encourage you as it's encouraged me and challenge you to step out in faith, no matter how crazy it seems.

KARI JOBE, Grammy-nominated worship artist

Dare to Be rekindles that fire dwelling inside you, reminding you that no matter what life throws at you, if you don't "dare to be," you'll never know what could have been.

SADIE ROBERTSON HUFF, author, speaker, and founder of *Live Original*

Encouraging. Hope-filled. Captivating. Charlotte and Natalie are the Jesus-focused big sisters we all need to navigate the uncharted territory God is welcoming us to step into. In this impactful, relatable, and truth-filled book, they equip us to disempower doubt from defining our decisions and allow faith to write our futures. She who dares, wins. Give this book to every woman you know!

SHELLEY GIGLIO, Passion City Church

A book about dreaming, daring, and believing that God can do more than we can imagine!

BOB GOFF, *New York Times* bestselling author

DA RE

— TO BE —

Charlotte Gambill & Natalie Grant

HARVEST HOUSE PUBLISHERS
EUGENE. OREGON

Cover design by Faceout Studio

Interior design and layout by KUHN Design Group

For bulk, special sales, or ministry purchases, please call 1-800-547-8979. Email: Customerservice@hhpbooks.com

M is a federally registered trademark of The Hawkins Children's LLC. Harvest House Publishers, Inc., is the exclusive licensee of the trademark.

Dare to Be
Copyright © 2021 by Charlotte Gambill and Natalie Grant
Published by Harvest House Publishers
Eugene, Oregon 97408
www.harvesthousepublishers.com

ISBN 978-0-7369-8456-0 (pbk.)
ISBN 978-0-7369-8457-7 (eBook)
ISBN 978-0-7369-8588-8 (eAudio)

Library of Congress Cataloging-in-Publication Data is on file at the Library of Congress, Washington, DC.

To our children:

Hope Cherish and Noah Brave
Grace Ana, Bella Noelle, and Sadie Rose

This is our story.

Your willingness to release is why we can dare to be.

This adventure is one that we all have had to take together.

From the moments our families collided, your hearts and lives also connected.

From doing bus life together to allowing us to kiss each
of you goodbye for a moment so we could be obedient
to go and help others in their moments of need.

Every salvation, transformation, and breakthrough
we have witnessed are ones we all share.

No words can express how much we love and cherish the most daring
of all adventures — raising such incredible world changers.

Our prayer is that you each would discover your own God-
filled journey, dare to make a difference, dare to dream for
something greater, and trust the One who holds your future.

Keep being true, kind, compassionate, and crazy. You are
our joy, and the best reward is coming home to you.

We love you always.

CONTENTS

I DARE YOU

dare you. Do you remember the first time you heard those words? We have all been dared by someone at some time. Perhaps someone at school dared you to be mischievous. Or maybe someone dared you to push beyond your previous achievements in a physical challenge.

We all respond differently to a dare. Some see it as an opportunity to prove themselves; others hear it as a challenge to their competence. Yet it's often the *I dare you* moments that push us beyond where comfort could keep us and the familiar would fence us in.

Such moments seem to appear more frequently when we are young, as part of our regular interactions with friends. As we get older, these conversations become less common; we become too mature to entertain something that seems so childish. But what if discarding the *I dare you* moments means we are keeping our potential hidden away within us? Perhaps the very thing we thought to be immature is what we need for our life *to* mature. What if the presence of the dare could open new doors for you?

When we read the Bible, we get a front-row seat to many *I dare you* moments of the past. God's Word is the record of those who went before us, the ones whom God used to forge the future through acts that were not for the fainthearted. The consistent theme of these accounts is a willingness to dare to go beyond the usual or normal: Moses before Pharaoh; Daniel in the lions' den; the disciples leaving behind all they knew to follow a man they had only just met.

Our present faith was shaped by those who dared in the past. Now it is our turn to dare to go farther and shape the future.

Perhaps it's time we all got back to the place of daring. A journey awaits those who, with courage and willingness, take the first steps on an uncharted path. For so long we've been safely managing our destinies, but it's time to make friends with the discomfort that comes when we choose to make God's words our security. The farther we go on the *I dare you* adventure with God, the more we discover His expansive capacity, His power and unfathomable ability. The more we see the One who works for us and in us—and who longs to work through us—the more we come to know His faithful and steadfast nature that never fails us.

Where fear has closed the door, we need the challenge of *I dare you* to open our lives to possibilities once more. Where we have held back because of doubt, we need to dare to trust and step out. Where we have stopped daring because we don't want to face failure, we need to allow the dare to deepen our learning and understanding.

Several years ago, some dear friends invited my husband and me to join them and a few of their friends—whom we had never met before—for a weekend of adventure. I was unsure about the invitation; I am much more of an introvert than the friend who was inviting us, and I didn't know how adventurous I would feel in a house full of strangers. However, we decided to take up the

The **I DARE YOU**

moments push us

beyond where

comfort could keep

us and the familiar

would fence us in.

challenge, and I dared to say yes. It was while we were away that I found myself going on my own journey of daring to be.

One afternoon we had been out on the water paddleboarding. As we came back to the dock, some of the group started to climb up a hillside to a diving ledge and leap off into the water below. I was very sure this was one activity I had no interest in doing. And then someone said these words: "I dare you."

My immediate internal response was, *No thank you!* But then I began to think, *When was the last time I took a dare?* This dare wasn't going to harm me, but it would stretch me. I am not a fan of heights—but what if this dare could help me face a fear that needed to be challenged?

As I started the ascent, I was so nervous and yet determined. I was reminded of something I had forgotten, a feeling I had left back in my youth—that nervous energy that stirs you to be a bit braver, a bit more courageous. I had my new friends at either side of me, holding my shaking arms as I stood on that board for well over ten minutes, trying to talk myself into jumping off. Everyone around me was cheering me on.

After what seemed like forever, I remember walking to the end of the board, holding my nose, and very ungracefully taking a leap into the water below. As I hit the water, everyone started applauding. I was so thankful it was over, but I had done it! Not that long before, I wouldn't have considered it a possibility. But I had leapt, and I had landed.

Perhaps it's time for you to start ascending into the dare that God has waiting for you. Perhaps it's time to face a fear or remove that area of limitation, to take the leap so you can land somewhere new. This book was written for you, so that you will hear a voice cheering you on—just like the voices of my newfound friends around me as I was on the ledge that day.

The very thing you are seeking could be on the other side of your daring. The leap you most fear may just be the leap you most need.

Don't allow fear to write

your future or lack to

limit your language.

What if you went on a journey of daring to be all God says you can be? What if you listened for His voice over every other voice? What if you discovered that the often-ignored nudges of the Spirit are dares to rise to something greater within you? It could be that some of the things you are praying for are not denied or delayed. Perhaps they are just disguised in the dares you are trying to avoid.

As you read through the chapters of this book, you will find the very honest account of two girls who embarked on a journey that began with a dare. We will share with you our highs and lows, the lessons and the moments that became pivotal for us as individuals and as friends. We are believing and praying that these pages will bring an impartation of God's Spirit—and that's why we want you not just to read each chapter, but also to write your own story. We invite you to take the same dares we took—to dare to believe, to begin, to build.

At the close of each chapter, Nat's notes will encourage you to devote that chapter's dare back to God. We invite you to read, to journal, to worship, to pray, and to embrace not just the words on the page, but the adventure that awaits. We are praying that as you open each chapter, the Holy Spirit will guide and nudge you when you need to pause, reflect, and maybe step into the unknown with your all-knowing God.

What if the best chapter of your life is yet to be written? What if the place where you have lived for so long was never meant to contain you, but to be a springboard that would increase and enlarge your life? What if you have yet to discover the greatest relationships, the most beautiful spaces, and the most exciting places where the vision becomes more vibrant and your story becomes more expansive? Consider what God has set out for us:

> By entering through faith into what God has always wanted to do
> for us—set us right with him, make us fit for him—we have it all

Our present faith

was shaped by those

who dared in the past.

Now it is our turn

to dare to go farther

and shape the future.

together with God because of our Master Jesus. And that's not all:
We throw open our doors to God and discover at the same moment
that he has already thrown open his door to us. We find ourselves
standing where we always hoped we might stand—out in the wide
open spaces of God's grace and glory, standing tall and shouting our
praise (Romans 5:1-2 MSG).

What wide-open space is waiting for you? Where do your walls need to come
down so creativity can flourish? Don't allow fear to write your future or lack to
limit your language. God is with you, friend, and He has already gone before
you. Perhaps your first dare is to commit afresh to the adventure of following
Him and trusting His plan over your own plan.

You were not born to live an ordinary life. You were considered so valuable,
you are so loved, that God sent His only Son for you, to die for you so that you
could truly live. You are surrounded by a great cloud of witnesses (Hebrews
12:1), and this is your turn, your time to dare to be all He has called you to be.

Take courage, friend, and together let's embrace the adventure that so often
begins with "I dare you."

1

DARE TO BE

Once upon a Time

Once upon a time... This is a phrase we are all familiar with. It's that mysterious introduction to an adventure. That moment in time when something first stirs, when the possibility begins to become something tangible. That phrase I would read out loud at the beginning of bedtime stories for my two children as they were growing up. It represents the intrigue, the questions, the potential about to unfold—because every great story starts somewhere.

The *once upon a time* in our stories becomes the place where we embark on some of the greatest journeys. For the next few moments, let's take a trip into the *once upon a time* that shaped the lives of two strangers. One that wasn't planned in either of their schedules. One that began a story they never imagined would design a new future in which to flourish.

This is the *once upon a time* of Dare to Be.

For some, Dare to Be may be familiar. For others who are joining this story for the first time, let's start at the very beginning. Let me take you back to 2005, on a summer's evening in a church auditorium in California. The event was a women's conference, and this was the opening night. The conference host had invited several guests to minister at this gathering, including a girl from England who taught the Word and a gospel singer from Nashville—by way of Seattle—who would lead some worship. These two girls had never met before. Actually, they did not even know of each other's existence. But both were about to be placed on the first page of God's story in their lives.

This is our *Dare to Be* story. Oh—by the way, I'm Charlotte, the English part of this equation, and the one who does most of the talking (on stage, that is). The American part—that's Natalie—takes care of all the singing. You'll hear from her a little further into these pages.

I had just unpacked in my hotel room. I was not speaking that evening, so I was very tempted to go to bed, as jet lag is not my friend. Yet for some reason, I decided I would go to the event that evening and just sit and enjoy the ministry that was going to take place.

I remember being a few rows from the front, standing and worshipping, caught up in the presence of God, when I was abruptly interrupted by an audible male voice. With my eyes still closed, I wondered if someone had come over to whisper some instruction to me about the conference. Was the conference host sending someone to get my attention? I opened my eyes, and no one was there—everyone was still worshipping. Then I heard the voice again, and what came next was the strangest instruction.

Before I share with you what I heard, I need to say something right from the start. When God is writing a *once upon a time* moment in our lives, He's the one who gets to control the script. The opening line is always His, and then the response is on us.

Often the first line of the chapter God wants to write can put us off. The start to the story leaves more questions than answers, requiring an element of bravery and daring from the very beginning. So when this voice gave me the strangest of instructions, I had to navigate all these uncertainties: *Is this really God speaking? Am I making this up? I'm probably just overtired.*

Sometimes our usual is challenged when it meets God's unusual. This reminds me of the story in 1 Samuel.

> One night Eli, whose eyes were becoming so weak that he could barely see, was lying down in his usual place. The lamp of God had not yet gone out, and Samuel was lying down in the house of the LORD, where the ark of God was. Then the LORD called Samuel.
>
> Samuel answered, "Here I am." And he ran to Eli and said, "Here I am; you called me."
>
> But Eli said, "I did not call; go back and lie down." So he went and lay down.
>
> Again the LORD called, "Samuel!" And Samuel got up and went to Eli and said, "Here I am; you called me."
>
> "My son," Eli said, "I did not call; go back and lie down."
>
> Now Samuel did not yet know the LORD: The word of the LORD had not yet been revealed to him.
>
> A third time the LORD called, "Samuel!" And Samuel got up and went to Eli and said, "Here I am; you called me."
>
> Then Eli realized that the LORD was calling the boy. So Eli told

Samuel, "Go and lie down, and if he calls you, say, 'Speak, LORD, for your servant is listening.'" So Samuel went and lay down in his place.

The LORD came and stood there, calling as at the other times, "Samuel! Samuel!"

Then Samuel said, "Speak, for your servant is listening" (1 Samuel 3:2-10).

Samuel was being mentored and trained by the older priest and servant of God, Eli. One night, this passage in 1 Samuel tells us, Samuel was asleep near the ark of God; the young boy was in proximity to God's presence, and it was in that place he found his *once upon a time* moment as God called to him.

Yet we are told that at first Samuel ran to Eli, thinking it was his voice calling for him to come. Eli, "in his usual place" (verse 2), couldn't hear what Samuel heard, so he dismissed him and sent him back to his sleep. This happened several times until Eli eventually realized this was God calling, and Samuel needed to respond. This was the part of Samuel's story where he needed to go and engage with God for himself.

Sometimes our "usual place" mentality can make us dismiss moments like the one I was about to experience that night in California. God tries to get our attention, and we just think, *It's nothing. It was just an idea. It wasn't significant.* But I have found some of the most significant moments often come disguised as some of the simplest acts of obedience.

Now, back to the worship meeting. I was in the presence of God, and I was realizing, *This is the voice of God.* As I opened my heart to listen, I heard something that made no sense.

Charlotte, open your eyes. The girl at the back of the auditorium in an orange sweater and jeans is to do with your future.

Our usual is

challenged when

it meets God's

unusual.

Yep, that was it. That was all I heard, and it was enough to completely freak me out. Surely it wasn't God—it was the jet lag. Surely I was imagining this. I had traveled to the event with a friend, and so my first response was not, *Yes, Lord. I believe You, Lord.* It was to elbow my friend who was worshipping next to me and say what must have seemed so random. I asked her to turn around and tell me if there was someone at the back of the auditorium in an orange sweater and jeans.

Let's just pause here for another moment. When God starts a *once upon a time*, it is never just about you. The story is going to involve a lot more characters along the way. He is going to use some in a moment of confirmation, and others will be part of the journey of bringing things together. I think now of that fast and fleeting confirmation I was asking someone to provide. Neither of us knew the significance of what was happening, and yet my friend willingly looked for a person in an orange sweater. It seemed like forever before her reply came, but eventually she whispered, "Yes, there's a girl at the door wearing an orange sweater and jeans." And of course, she followed that up with, "Why do you want to know?"

"Don't ask," I replied. Yes, I was embarrassed to say the words that I had felt God whisper to me. This completely random person, whom I hadn't even turned around and acknowledged for myself, had something to do with my future. It seemed silly to even think that, let alone say it out loud.

It was just after this that the worship came to an end. A big part of me wanted to turn around, but I decided to carry on as if nothing had happened. I mean, you don't just invite people into your future. How would you even start that conversation? "Hello, total stranger. I like your sweater, and by the way, you will be a part of my future." Exactly. It sounds ridiculous. Then there were the other thoughts that were going on in my mind—*Is it really the girl in* this *sweater? I think it looks more peach than orange.*

You can see where I was going. Embracing your *once upon a time* is a lot more complicated than the fairy tales let on. How many times have you had a thought that seems so strange to your mind and yet your heart is pounding? But you don't dare to follow the prompting. The Bible is full of moments like this. Let's consider the disciples on the road to Emmaus.

> Now that same day two of them were going to a village called Emmaus, about seven miles from Jerusalem. They were talking with each other about everything that had happened. As they talked and discussed these things with each other, Jesus himself came up and walked along with them; but they were kept from recognizing him (Luke 24:13-16).

These two disciples had left Jerusalem; they were heartbroken after Jesus' death. They had heard about the resurrection, but they couldn't believe the good news. Even though Jesus had told them what was going to happen and had instructed them that a new story was about to begin, their doubts took them on a detour. When Jesus in His resurrected body decided to join their walk and engage in their rather depressing conversation, they had a heart-pounding moment.

> When [Jesus] was at the table with them, he took bread, gave thanks, broke it and began to give it to them. Then their eyes were opened and they recognized him, and he disappeared from their sight. They asked each other, "Were not our hearts burning within us while he talked with us on the road and opened the Scriptures to us?" (Luke 24:30-32).

In other words, they knew it was not just anybody who had talked with them. They knew that conversation was not like any other. They had sensed in their hearts that this was Jesus, and yet they had never committed to actually saying what they felt. This can happen to all of us. We can miss moments because we want more information—and yet, as we all know, the best fairy tales require more belief than evidence.

So here I was with this burning feeling that God was speaking, but in a complete dilemma because of how ridiculous it all seemed. Surely the best thing to do was just ignore it and carry on as normal? Well, that's what I attempted to do until another player in this story stepped in.

I am taking the time to record each moment of this *once upon a time* becoming a reality because I want to acknowledge every part that was played. God uses all of us in one another's lives; we are needed to keep the story in motion. Sometimes you get a leading role, at other times a supporting role. And here's the thing: All these roles are vitally important.

Remember Paul's conversion and Ananias playing his part (Acts 9:10-19)? Without his willingness to meet with Saul the persecutor, the next part of Paul's story could not unfold. Remember the boy who gave his lunch (John 6:5-13)? He could have thought, *Why offer something that seems so insignificant?* He could have seen the disciples and the people around Jesus and disqualified himself from being able to approach them, never mind offering his lunch as part of the solution. Yet his supporting role became central to the miracle of feeding 5,000. So let's not rush past this next moment as God used several people to get this *once upon a time* established.

As worship ended, I took my seat and was busy trying to ignore what had just happened when the host of the conference tapped me on the shoulder. I had known this lovely lady for years, and she is one of those sweet people who is soft spoken and so gentle in her manner. She simply touched my shoulder and said, "I know you're not speaking tonight, but it would be lovely if you could stand up and greet people and lead the giving part of the service."

Here's the thing about sweet and gentle people: It's hard to say no to them. So I agreed to an impromptu role in taking the offering, which clearly was not as impromptu as I thought.

As I was leaving my chair she added, "Oh, just one thing. The giving leads into a time of worship. Could you introduce our guest who'll be singing?"

Now you have to understand that all those years back, Christian music was pretty much nonexistent in England; we didn't have Christian television or music channels, so most gospel singers and worship artists were unknown to me. When I was asked to introduce the singer, I was a little torn. I was sure this person was amazing, but how was I supposed to introduce someone I had never heard of? I didn't want to appear insincere, and yet I wanted to serve the host in the best way possible.

In a quick scramble for information, a team member handed me the singer's bio and said, "When you get to that part, just read this out. She'll come on and sing."

Here I was, confused at the whole orange sweater thing, now preparing to ask people to bring their offerings—oh, and then introduce a person I had never heard of. God's *once upon a times* require a lot of simple and yet not-so-simple steps of obedience. You never know; your *yes* may be the entrance point to the adventure you have been longing for.

When it was time to read the bio as I stood on stage, I began with the first line: "We are so excited tonight to have with us an incredible gospel singer." I said the words with as much enthusiasm as I could when I had no idea who I was talking about—and I became distracted by someone moving. I looked up and saw, walking from the back of the auditorium down the center aisle, the girl in the orange sweater and jeans. I was talking, she was walking toward me, and then, well, the whole room got to witness a beautiful and God-planned interruption.

Your **YES** *may be*

the entrance

point to the

adventure you

have been longing for.

I opened my mouth to read the next line of the bio, and what came out was not what was written on the paper but what was written on God's page. I started prophesying words over the stranger in the aisle, and she started crying—as these were words her heart clearly needed to hear. I honestly can't remember what I said, and perhaps that's just how God meant it to be. Those words were for her heart and not for my holding. All I know is that this stranger in the orange sweater was moving closer, not just in physical proximity but also somehow spiritually.

As she made it up onto the platform to try to sing in front of everyone who had just witnessed her tears, I remember giving her a very awkward hug. I whispered, "I'm Charlotte, and I don't know what's happening. I don't normally do this."

She whispered, "I'm Natalie, and I don't either."

With that I left the stage and took my seat, and then the girl in the orange sweater closed her eyes and opened her mouth and, well, that's when my tears started flowing. There was such anointing, such purity, such power in the words she sang. And in some very strange way, there was such familiarity in the place from which these words were being drawn.

Once upon a time, two strangers from two different nations, two girls who didn't know each other, were somehow on the same page. I knew something was happening, but I had no idea what it was. Just as when you read the first page of a fairy tale, and you are intrigued to know what is going to happen, the next chapter beckoned. This was the *once upon a time* of Dare to Be.

NOTES FROM NATALIE

Hi. I'm Natalie, the girl in the orange sweater and jeans. Throughout this book, I'll be bringing our thoughts together at the end of each chapter. We wanted you not just to read but to pause and absorb what God may want to write on the page of your heart. Let's keep turning our eyes toward heaven and listening for His voice, taking the lessons we have learned for encouragement and strength on our individual journeys. Let's take a moment to reflect and devote this time back to God together. For this chapter, I'd like to use the lyrics of my song "Awaken" to guide these devotional thoughts.

Let me start by telling you that 2005, the year I met Charl, was a pivotal year in my life. It was a time when, looking back, I can see God was really trying to get my attention. It was the year I became aware of human trafficking and set up my nonprofit Hope for Justice. It was the year I heard that my husband and I might never be able to have children. It was the year my album *Awaken* was released, which really changed things in terms of my career. And of course there was that night in the auditorium in California. It was like God was stirring everything up so I couldn't ignore His greater purpose.

I'm sure you also have had times like this. Perhaps you are experiencing this kind of awakening right now. You might feel a little out of control, that there is a lot going on that is not part of your plan. That's because God wants more for you than just to exist. He wants you to live for Him.

We can have this idea of our identity—and for me all those years ago, it was, *I'm a singer; I'm a songwriter.* That's it, no room for anything else. We can all try to categorize our life: *I am made to do this, and I am made to do that.* We think of that one thing as an arrival point. We put so much emphasis on our dreams, instead of realizing we can be awakened to our true identity, to our true purpose. God's *once upon a time* is the greatest story ever told, and this is our purpose: to tell the story of who Jesus is.

In the song "Awaken," I invite God to take control. He has so much more for us when we allow Him to lead, when we stop plotting and planning our future and allow Him to show us our destiny. When we relinquish control and

God wants more

for you than just

to exist. He wants

you to live for Him.

let all the paths of our lives intersect—our careers, our relationships, our families—we are no longer just heading to a destination. Instead, we are embarking on a journey toward our destiny in Christ.

Our purpose is to tell the greater story. Take a few moments to read the lyrics of this song, making them your prayer. In what area of your life do you need to pray, *Wake me up, Lord?* Where do you need to allow His power and passion to take the pen and write your next page?

As we close this first chapter, we pray you would take the time to allow God to stir your own story so that all you do brings Him glory.

Sometimes I feel like I'm just existing
I'm not really living
I'm only watching the time slip away
I've forgotten who I am in You
I'm not who I'm meant to be
I'm drifting farther away from my destiny

Awaken my heart, awaken my soul
Awaken Your power and take control
Awaken the passion to live for You, Lord
Awaken me

Open my eyes so I can see
Your presence dwelling inside
Wake me up, 'cause I can't live
Another minute if I'm not shining Your light

Awaken my heart, awaken my soul
Awaken the passion in me
Lord, awaken me to live my destiny[1]

QUESTIONS FOR DISCUSSION AND REFLECTION

- In which situations or places has comfort contained you in the past?

- In what areas of your life do you want to embark on new adventures?

- What godly promptings do you need to give more attention to?

2

DARE TO BELIEVE

The worship song ended and, just like that, the girl in the orange sweater exited the stage with her team and left the room. Back in my seat I was hemmed in by people on every side. As the speaker took to the platform, I knew it would be rude to try to leave the auditorium. If this were a fairy tale, the singer would be Cinderella, running out of the great hall to get home before midnight. She didn't even leave her slipper behind.

Of course I didn't have the girl's phone number, as we had only just met, and our meeting was on a very public platform where there was no time or opportunity for us to exchange contact information. I had no idea where she was going or if she was even staying in town. As I was trying to pay attention to the word that was being ministered, my mind was doing mental gymnastics as I tried to figure out my next steps. I'd appointed myself the architect of what would happen next.

Isn't that just like us? God does something miraculous, He starts the story, and then we want to try to help Him get it written in a way we feel would be most efficient. I had figured out I could ask the conference host for the details of her guest singer, and I could write a note asking if we could have some kind of conversation. Yet the more I thought about it, the more awkward it started feeling. This God-breathed first page was about to be followed by a very poorly written chapter if I was going to try to control the story.

It reminds me of the powerful introduction of a young man called David. For all his life, David had been unseen and overlooked as he watched sheep. Yet he was about to have a *once upon a time* moment of his own when God brought David down to the front lines of the battle.

> Now Jesse said to his son David, "Take this ephah of roasted grain and these ten loaves of bread for your brothers and hurry to their camp. Take along these ten cheeses to the commander of their unit. See how your brothers are and bring back some assurance from them" (1 Samuel 17:17-18).

Let's just take a moment to appreciate the way that God began the most epic adventure of David's life. It all started with bread and cheese. David had to be willing to run an errand if he wanted to discover the next part of his story, which was waiting in the form of a challenger named Goliath.

How often do we want the Goliath-defeating moment but not the errand—the unseen, thankless task that precedes victory? We don't want to be seen as the bread-and-cheese person, and yet it was only through that obedience in serving his brothers—who viewed him as insignificant—that David ended up in the place where everybody wanted to be.

How many bread distribution opportunities have we turned down because we are waiting for something that sounds so much more exciting? The test of *daring to be* isn't just in the big things; it's in the little things too. It's daring to be faithful when you are asked to run the errand, just as much as it is being fiercely courageous when you need to face the giant.

The errand David was asked to run by his father became the start of an adventure no one had planned. The youngest brother delivered the food, but so much more was about to happen; the story of a great king was about to begin.

When David saw Goliath, he sensed the nudge to step into the story. The simplicity of a sling and a stone was all God needed to write a first page that would get everyone's attention. As soon as the giant was slain, however, others tried to dictate what should come next; King Saul, who was jealous and insecure, wanted to control the script of David's life. Even David's family had previously tried to seize control of his story—they'd wanted to exclude him from his own anointing party! (See 1 Samuel 16:1-13.)

People who love you can have a tendency to want to control such pivotal moments. When you start to leave the preferred script that others have selected for your future, you may find you have a lot of editors showing up. They want to tidy up your story so it can get back to the chapter they would prefer to see written for your future.

Often God's introduction can be hijacked by chapter two of everyone else's opinion. That's why, when you are daring to be, you have to dare to believe. David believed God was with him and, therefore, when he was offered an alternative script, he was secure enough to turn it down. When you know God was the One who started the story, you would much rather that He keep writing.

The challenge here is that we have to believe beyond our need to be in control. Up until this point of the story of Dare to Be, I was not in control—but now, in that auditorium, I realized I could be. So as I sat with my notebook, I considered the different options of what I could do next.

When the conference session ended, we were taken to an area in the building where some refreshments were being served. I chatted with people and then suddenly noticed that orange sweater again. (Oddly enough, as Natalie will tell you, orange is not her color, and she has never worn an orange sweater again.

Maybe that's not her color—or maybe she is a little nervous to put that sweater on again in case she meets another random stranger. One English invasion is enough for anyone!)

When I spotted Natalie, I decided to go over and officially introduce myself. I first apologized for making her cry before she sang and tried to explain that this was not how I normally behaved.

She very sweetly listened and then said, "You know, that *was* really strange—and yet the words you delivered were exactly what I needed to hear." I gave a sigh of relief. At least I knew that was God speaking and not the jet lag. And then she said something else: "Can I ask what you want from me?"

It seemed a strange thing to ask, but I would later realize it was a question that came from an ache in her heart. I replied, "I don't know what you mean. I don't want anything—honestly. I live in England, and I'm heading home after this event to run my women's conference next month."

Natalie paused, then said, "I think I need to come and bring my husband."

My conference, which is called Cherish and is usually held in a huge arena, was at an early stage then and held in our church building. It's in a part of the United Kingdom few people travel to; it's not in London or a major city, and there are no castles or palaces near our church building. I was so shocked when she said she wanted to come that I replied, "Well, I can't afford to add any guests at this point."

She looked at me and smiled. She said, "Not to sing. I just think I need to come."

It was then I realized that my best attempt at writing chapter two was so poor compared to what God was writing. It wasn't until much later that I discovered just how burned out this girl in the orange sweater was. She was constantly being asked to be somewhere and do something. She was tired, and she was a little hesitant to believe in the possibility of a relationship that went beyond what people saw on a stage to someone who would just love her for who she was.

I didn't know quite how big the step of believing was for Natalie that day. She had decided not to jump on the tour bus and head back on the road with her band. She had held everyone back as she waited for me to come into that room so she could see what God was going to write next in her story. Neither of us had a clue what was happening, and yet both of us had to believe that God was up to something.

Believing in what we can see is one thing, but believing in the unknown is a whole different level of daring to be. That day, Natalie was choosing to believe that we needed to take another step. As she chose to believe God was in this, she became vulnerable enough for the next chapter to begin.

In just a few minutes, some huge decisions were about to be made. Two strangers were about to agree to get together, a meeting that had no real clarity but did have a cost and time attached to it. You can say you believe God is in something, but committing to get on an airplane and fly across an ocean moves believing into reality. That's the kind of faith God is looking for. As James 2:26 reminds us, "As the body without the spirit is dead, so faith without deeds is dead."

That's the power of faith and deeds, that our believing gets real when we start the journey of doing. When we say *yes* and then book the ticket; when we say *amen* and then step into the opportunity.

Within a few moments a trip was planned; Natalie was going to come to England, and she was going to bring her husband (who at this point had no idea any of this was happening) and visit me and my husband (who was in another time zone, oblivious to what was being planned). It seemed crazy, and yet there was this sense that the crazy was exactly what God required to get chapter two on paper.

Believing gets real

when we start the

journey of doing.

Every time Nat and I remember this moment, we're simply amazed. Anyone who knows us would say we are more planners than spontaneous, more cautious than careless. In fact, years later Nat told me that when she and her husband got on the plane, she said to him, "This woman could be completely mad, and if she is, we are *out* of there. But at least we'll get a vacation in England out of it."

We laugh when we think about it, but that's what believing does. It gets you making decisions you normally wouldn't, thinking of options you never would have considered. For us, there was such a belief in the hand of God on the page that we knew to try and take over the story now would cause us to miss crucial parts of the plot.

The Bible talks often about our role as followers of Christ. We can give an *amen* in agreement to this…but it's not always as simple to follow Christ as it sounds. If a friend takes the lead when you're planning to drive somewhere, she might say, "Just follow me." You jump in your car and get behind her. You can see her car ahead of you; you can see her turn signal indicating the next turn. It's easy to keep following.

I would love to tell you that's what following Jesus is like. There are moments when the indication is clear and the direction is evident, but there are also times when the road gets busy and there is a lot of traffic in the way. Then it becomes harder to tail that vehicle in front.

When our lives get busy, following gets harder. And in that moment, though Natalie and I were both busy—the tour bus waiting, the room full of guests wanting to say hello, the team asking if we would like more food—we couldn't let those distractions get in the way of our believing. Instead, we cleared the freeway. Neither of us checked our calendars, even though we both knew our schedules didn't have room for a trip. Our hearts believed the Way Maker was making a way.

Returning to the story of David, we see another character awakening to the journey of daring. A prince named Jonathan heard his father, Saul, talking to David, and he knew in that moment that God was doing something. He felt his spirit respond to what didn't make sense in his mind.

> After David had finished talking with Saul, Jonathan became one in spirit with David, and he loved him as himself. From that day Saul kept David with him and did not let him return home to his family. And Jonathan made a covenant with David because he loved him as himself. Jonathan took off the robe he was wearing and gave it to David, along with his tunic, and even his sword, his bow and his belt (1 Samuel 18:1-4).

Jonathan believed that God was leading his life down a path that no one else would have suggested. For Jonathan to serve David, he had to believe that God held his future—and that trust needed to be deeper than his feelings of entitlement as an heir to the throne. Jonathan, who had the kingdom as his inheritance, should have seen David as a potential threat. But he dared to let go of what was rightfully his. He forsook the well-written plans for his future in exchange for something far less clear on paper but so very clear in his spirit.

For us, in that back room in California, a decision was made within moments that ordinarily would have taken months—if not years. Two strangers took the next step, which would involve a lot of administration and rearranging and an investment of time and money. I think that's why a lot of great stories never really get started. It's fun when God's clearly making something happen, but when you have to work to keep the story going, it seems less exciting and far riskier.

Tickets and hotel rooms had to be booked. The passing awkward conversation might become a lot more awkward as we spent a prolonged time together.

There was a lot more investment than there was information. Yet somehow, our shared belief was down payment enough.

That first evening and that first conversation came to an end, and Natalie left town. Now another layer of believing had to happen. The decision we had just made would need to be explained to people who weren't there in the room but whose lives would be impacted by our *yes*.

I remember calling my husband, Steve, when the time zones permitted. Our conversation went something like, "Hey babe, I met this girl last night in an orange sweater. God says she's to do with my future, so she's coming to England with her husband next month and we are going to look after them." Yep, that was about all I could say. My husband then had to process his response to this next chapter that had begun without him being aware the page had turned.

As I was trying to tell Steve about all this, Natalie was doing the same thing with her husband, Bernie. It's hard enough to get your own faith ready to step out, never mind having to share that preparation with others. That's why sometimes we need to realize that when people share their heart and dreams with us, our words may need to be less so God can keep doing more.

When Zechariah was visited by an angel in the book of Luke, he was told the news he and his wife, Elizabeth, had longed to hear for many years—news that she would carry a child. The *once upon a time* was about to begin, and now Zechariah just had to respond and dare to believe. Yet in his shock, the facts of the situation seemed to overwhelm his faith for the future. He received this news from the angel not with belief, but with a question.

> An angel of the Lord appeared to him, standing at the right side of the altar of incense. When Zechariah saw him, he was startled and was gripped with fear. But the angel said to him: "Do not be afraid,

Zechariah; your prayer has been heard. Your wife Elizabeth will bear
you a son, and you are to call him John."…

Zechariah asked the angel, "How can I be sure of this? I am an old
man and my wife is well along in years" (Luke 1:11-13,18).

What happened next may seem a little extreme, but I think it requires our
attention. Our words are often more critical than we realize. See how the angel
responded to Zechariah's disbelief.

The angel said to him, "I am Gabriel. I stand in the presence of God,
and I have been sent to speak to you and to tell you this good news.
And now you will be silent and not able to speak until the day this
happens, because you did not believe my words, which will come
true at their appointed time" (Luke 1:19-20).

In an instant, Zechariah was silenced. He left the presence of the angel
unable to speak, which meant he was unable to spread his disbelief to his wife.
Perhaps God wanted to protect Elizabeth from the derailment of unbeliev-
ing conversations, and the silencing of her husband's fear meant Elizabeth was
able to believe and find faith. The silencing of doubts in her immediate circle
created an incubator for possibility. The step she was embarking on was hard
enough—carrying the child she had given up hoping for—without the questioning of someone she loved.

However, God didn't leave Elizabeth all alone. Just as God helped remove
the wrong voice, He also sent the right voice into her life. Like what God did
for David, when He replaced the critical voices of his brothers with a devoted
new brother in the form of Jonathan. God silenced Zechariah's doubts and sent
to Elizabeth's side Mary, who was also at the start of her own *once upon a time*.

Mary went to her relative Elizabeth's house, because there she knew she would find a friend for this chapter of her story—one who would not only encourage her, but also believe alongside her what God had put in motion. Both were having to dare to believe.

> At that time Mary got ready and hurried to a town in the hill country of Judea, where she entered Zechariah's home and greeted Elizabeth. When Elizabeth heard Mary's greeting, the baby leaped in her womb, and Elizabeth was filled with the Holy Spirit. In a loud voice she exclaimed: "Blessed are you among women, and blessed is the child you will bear! But why am I so favored, that the mother of my Lord should come to me? As soon as the sound of your greeting reached my ears, the baby in my womb leaped for joy. Blessed is she who has believed that the Lord would fulfill his promises to her!" (Luke 1:39-45).

How kind is God to put people in our story who will believe with us? When such people enter your story, they help you believe in what you are called to carry.

Mary entered Elizabeth's home, and the baby inside Elizabeth leapt for joy. Zechariah's unbelief was replaced with what God had already placed in the wings. In your own daring, don't stop in the face of other people's unbelief. Instead, trust that God will place an *amen* in people who see what you see, even if they were not there when it was revealed.

Thankfully, neither of our husbands ended up struck mute like Zechariah. Both of them were a little shocked that the usually careful and unspontaneous wives they knew so well were suggesting something that seemed so out of left field, but maybe that's why it was easier for them to believe and dare with us.

The next page doesn't get written unless we dare to believe. There are too

The believing has

to come even before

the beginning.

many unanswered questions for logic to write and too many risks for caution to approve. The believing has to come even before the beginning. Natalie and I had no idea what we were going to do when we met up in England. Would we even get along? But we were very aware that the next chapter was underway, and the One we believed held the pen.

NOTES FROM NATALIE

God took care of so many details so Charl and I could meet. My orange sweater helped me stand out in the crowd enough for her to notice me. God ensured that I could clear my schedule to make a trip to England when Charl was hosting her conference. Our husbands didn't think we were crazy when we shared about our encounter. Sometimes it is easier to believe God for the big than it is to trust Him for the small. But in these details, He revealed to us both that the all-powerful God is also our very personal Father and Friend.

God knows exactly what we need, even if we don't know how to ask for these things. We can go on with our day-to-day, not expecting God to do any more than the familiar, not believing for increase because we have settled for what we have. In this way, we can exclude ourselves from the story God has for us, feeling we are insignificant. *Why*, we ask, *would the God of all space and time notice and be bothered with me?*

When you feel you are at this place and hiding yourself away, remember that just as God showed up in our story, He is working in yours too. My song "Do It Through Me" has become my response to this realization that God wants to involve me, that He notices me, that He cares about what I care about. I can't believe God would want to work through me; I can't believe He would choose someone like me, someone who may slip and fall.

Charl and I didn't have it all together when God began our Dare to Be journey—and we still don't—but God took our willingness to serve Him as the starting point for the next chapter He was stirring. We had to dare to believe in His power, recognizing that there is no limit to what He can do in and through us.

This is the personal side of our God. He is relational with us, and the amazing thing is, we all have His DNA. We are His children, and He chooses to accomplish His purposes through us. What an awesome thing that a God so big would trust us with His divine work.

As we close out this chapter, we want to encourage you to dare to believe He wants to use someone just like you. He sees and He knows, so use the lyrics from this song to focus your devotional time. Let your heart say back to God, the author and finisher of all our stories, *I'm Yours to be used.*

You look to the weak and You reach for the small
Trust them in places they might slip and fall
It's hard to believe
But, Lord, I believe

So I keep on 'cause You keep on givin' me grace
When I walk in Your will, when I'm runnin' Your race
'Cause You are the King and I'm Yours to be used
It's just hard to believe I'm somebody You'd choose

Who am I that I have Your DNA?
Who am I that You'd let me wear Your name?
That You wanna use me
Who am I that You'd let me play a part?
Who am I that You'd shine me in the dark?
But You wanna use me[2]

QUESTIONS FOR DISCUSSION AND REFLECTION

- What is it time to believe in again?

- What lies can you replace with God's truth?

- What do you believe and hope for that will stretch your faith in the future?

_____

_____

_____

_____

_____

_____

_____

_____

_____

_____

3

DARE TO BE REAL

So the plane tickets were booked and two people I did not know—one whom I had never met—were on their way over the ocean to England. This was either going to be a comedy of errors or the start of a great adventure. I would like to say I was fully convinced it would be the latter, but with so many unknowns, I was more aware of what could go wrong than what could go right.

As I mentioned in the previous chapter, many potentially great stories get dismissed at this stage—struggling to know whether we should begin, procrastinating on finding out more information, stalling while looking for more signs. Our insecurities and doubt are like adding extra weight to our luggage before a flight.

At the airport, bags are weighed with restrictions placed on the amount of luggage you can bring onboard. If you are overloaded, you might have to choose what you are going to leave behind if you want to take off for your destination. Similarly, some of the destinations God wants you to embrace require you to lighten the load. The questions, the second-guessing, the list of things you think you need—they won't be permitted in the luggage allowance for this adventure.

I remember one time when I was flying home from the United States, a family several places in front of me in line reached the check-in counter. As their large bags were being weighed, they were informed by the staff that they would have to pay a large penalty if they wanted to bring all that extra weight onboard. So the family excused themselves from the desk and moved to the side, just opposite where I was waiting in line. They then proceeded to open every suitcase as one of the parents instructed each member of the family to add several layers of clothing. They began putting sweaters on top of sweaters and even trousers over trousers. As you can imagine, this brought great amusement to their growing audience. They then went back to the same check-in agent and presented their lighter bags while looking like much heavier people.

This can happen to our hearts. We can be so reluctant to let go of things, even though we know they don't belong in our future. We try to get inventive in the way we smuggle onboard the stowaways and backup plans that God has asked us to jettison. I think the start of new adventures presents this opportunity to all of us—the possibility of leaving some things behind that were once a part of our story but no longer should be.

God gave Lot and his wife an opportunity to start a new chapter. They had a chance to leave their past behind and enter a future that was filled with hope.

> With the coming of dawn, the angels urged Lot, saying, "Hurry! Take your wife and your two daughters who are here, or you will be swept away when the city is punished."
>
> When he hesitated, the men grasped his hand and the hands of his wife and of his two daughters and led them safely out of the city, for the LORD was merciful to them. As soon as they had brought them

out, one of them said, "Flee for your lives! Don't look back, and don't stop anywhere in the plain! Flee to the mountains or you will be swept away!" (Genesis 19:15-17).

All they had to do was let go of what had no part in their new beginning… and yet Lot's wife couldn't help but look back.

> By the time Lot reached Zoar, the sun had risen over the land. Then the LORD rained down burning sulfur on Sodom and Gomorrah—from the LORD out of the heavens. Thus he overthrew those cities and the entire plain, destroying all those living in the cities—and also the vegetation in the land. But Lot's wife looked back, and she became a pillar of salt (Genesis 19:23-26).

Letting go of what has been can leave us with a sense of uncertainty and apprehension. Lot and his family knew there were better days ahead, but somehow, the grip of what had become their normal was so strong for Lot's wife that she hesitated in the place where she should have kept moving. She focused on what was behind and, in so doing, lost her chance to discover what was ahead.

The same happened for the children of Israel. They had become so attached to the bondage of their past that, at the entrance to a new life of liberty, they began to lament over what they had left. They questioned the worth of the journey and doubted the purpose of going any farther. They even ended up painting a mental picture of their place of captivity as if it were a place of great provision and blessing. They remembered food they once ate but somehow forgot the chains in which they'd had to eat.

> In the desert the whole community grumbled against Moses and Aaron. The Israelites said to them, "If only we had died by the

Lord's hand in Egypt! There we sat around pots of meat and ate all the food we wanted, but you have brought us out into this desert to starve this entire assembly to death" (Exodus 16:2-3).

The enemy specializes in these moments; he makes sure you look at the post-cards from the past with a nostalgia that masks the reality, so you never seek the invitation to new adventures and greater liberty. Satan has a vested interest in ensuring the stories God wants to help you write stay unfinished.

When the enemy senses your boldness and your commitment to begin, he gets busy sending you postcards to encourage you to hold back, look back, and eventually turn back. That's why, at this point in the process, you have to dare to be real—real about what that last chapter really felt like, real about your reluctance to leave that time behind, and real enough to begin what's next without any of the baggage that should remain in the past.

The plane journey Natalie and her husband were taking was a trip to a new, never-before-visited destination—not just physically, but, as was increasingly evident, also spiritually. The environment presented—in both the natural and the spiritual sense—new sights to see, new people to meet, a new climate to adjust to, and new things to taste and experience. There was no one who knew them at this new destination, so no preconceived ideas, labels, roles, or demands were waiting to be fulfilled.

This was a blank piece of paper, and often it's such pages that we find most intimidating. Sometimes it's easier to go and be who people want us to be, to fulfill the image they have in their minds of how we should act. Blank pages can cause us to feel insecure, and yet it's often those pages that serve as the starting point for our greatest discoveries of who we can dare to be.

Dare to be real enough

to begin what's next

without any of the

baggage that should

remain in the past.

SHOW UP AS YOURSELF

When we first meet people, we try to present the best dressed, most polished versions of ourselves. We tuck in our insecurity and cover our nerves. We camouflage our doubts and even make our brilliance less bold. Like someone on a first date, we try to present the image we think will secure a second date.

Such feelings were at the forefront of my mind when it came to how these days with Natalie would look. What did I need to do to ensure I wouldn't be seen as crazy? What could I do to look less nervous or seem more professional? Yet the best stories are not the ones where you pretend to be someone else. The best adventures take place when you are fully present and fully *you*, when the baggage is left at the door and the conversation begins not with all you do, but who you are.

When Jesus met the disciples for the first time, He invited them to leave some baggage behind. He invited them to embrace a new reality within them. He invited these fishermen to fish for people. Jesus wanted them to become more of who He knew they were destined to be, even though that would require leaving a business and place of security. This new calling would require them to visit unknown places and be introduced all over again.

Perhaps you've had the experience of following someone on Instagram and then meeting them in real life. Were you confused? Perhaps the image they had presented online didn't match the reality. When we don't dare to be real, we let teachers tell us who we are or who we are not; we allow failed relationships to tell us we need to improve the version of ourselves we present to the world. We can let mistakes and past hurts point us to a very different future than what God intends. That's why, when it comes to the arrival of a new opportunity, I am appealing for the real *you* to show up and leave all the other versions at the door.

New chapters invite us to become a little more of who we really are. They give us an opportunity for a fresh introduction to the world around us. Often we need to go away from what has become too familiar to find what we need to discover. Jesus wasn't able to carry the story of His journey in Nazareth because familiarity prevented the people from seeing the reality of who He was.

> Jesus left there and went to his hometown, accompanied by his disciples. When the Sabbath came, he began to teach in the synagogue, and many who heard him were amazed.
>
> "Where did this man get these things?" they asked. "What's this wisdom that has been given him? What are these remarkable miracles he is performing? Isn't this the carpenter? Isn't this Mary's son and the brother of James, Joseph, Judas and Simon? Aren't his sisters here with us?" And they took offense at him.
>
> Jesus said to them, "A prophet is not without honor except in his own town, among his relatives and in his own home." He could not do any miracles there, except lay his hands on a few sick people and heal them (Mark 6:1-5).

All those people let a familiar face obscure the real miracle, excluding themselves from the reality of Immanuel—"God with us" (Matthew 1:23)—the Messiah present among them. Let's not make the same mistake. Let's not miss what God is doing and how He is moving because we're too stuck in the familiar.

I dare you to be real. I dare you to take off any masks or costumes that life has handed you. Perhaps you've sought to attain a superhero cape, an impressive title, or eye-catching attire to cover wounds you'd rather not display. But if you want the God adventure, if you want the deeper revelation, then the real *you* must step up.

Naaman was an impressive warrior. When he entered a town, the people feared him and revered his presence. Yet in reality Naaman was hiding his weakness underneath all the layers of his wealth and status; he was a man who was in need of healing.

> Naaman was commander of the army of the king of Aram. He was a great man in the sight of his master and highly regarded, because through him the LORD had given victory to Aram. He was a valiant soldier, but he had leprosy (2 Kings 5:1).

The help he needed came in the form of a young servant girl in his household. She was close enough to Naaman to see the reality beneath the veneer—the disease that had ravaged his body. The real Naaman was ill and scared, and this servant girl, whose role was to be more in the background than the foreground, took a step that required boldness. She suggested that her master seek help from the prophet Elisha.

Elisha told Naaman the steps he must take to receive the healing he so desperately wanted. Those steps felt like impossible leaps for Naaman, who was now faced with how he wanted this story to read: to carry on as the impressive military hero, or to go to a river where everyone could see his brokenness and dip under the water until he found a place of wholeness.

> Elisha sent a messenger to say to him, "Go, wash yourself seven times in the Jordan, and your flesh will be restored and you will be cleansed."
>
> But Naaman went away angry and said, "I thought that he would surely come out to me and stand and call on the name of the LORD his God, wave his hand over the spot and cure me of my leprosy. Are

not Abana and Pharpar, the rivers of Damascus, better than all the waters of Israel? Couldn't I wash in them and be cleansed?" So he turned and went off in a rage (2 Kings 5:10-12).

The choice between being well and staying sick may seem obvious, but sometimes we are more attached to our image than we are to our breakthrough. This is why the start of a new chapter will always present the challenge of daring to be real. Your best story requires you to be *you*. And that's what happened next in our story. Two people were about to dare to get real in the most unusual of ways.

OPEN THE DOOR

A few days after Nat arrived in the United Kingdom, I suggested she join me and a few friends for lunch and a visit to some clothing stores. I knew if we didn't have enough to talk about, shopping could be our instant way to bond.

In one of the stores, Nat went into a changing room to try on a few items. After a while I sensed that nudge again, like God was still writing this script—and somehow I was missing my prompt to enter stage left. So I came around the corner to face the changing room I knew Nat had entered. I knocked awkwardly on the door and said, "Hey, you okay in there?"

There was a pause, and then I heard a short reply. "Yep, I'm fine."

Something inside me knew that wasn't the answer she wanted to give. So I waited a moment and then knocked again. "Can I come in?" I asked. I had no idea whether she was in the middle of changing into a new outfit or ready to leave.

She let me in, and there she sat on the floor of the changing room. Laid out in front of her were needles and vials. She was shaking and looked flustered… and yet, in the same moment, a little relieved I had barged in. When I again asked if she was okay, she gave the answer she had wanted to give all along: "No."

Nat began to explain how right before they had left the United States, she and her husband had started treatments to help her get pregnant. After years of trying for a baby, they were told that they couldn't conceive naturally, and they were now beginning the course of treatment the doctors had advised as the best option to help improve their fertility.

She described how she had to give herself injections and how the treatment schedule had fallen on the days she and her husband were in England. She had to bring all the medication with her, and because the treatment was supposed to be administered on a time line set by her doctor in the United States, the change in time zones was not working well for her. While she was in the changing room, the alarm had started beeping to alert her that now was the time to have her injection—something she had never actually done to herself yet.

In this most awkward of settings, she felt overwhelmed and embarrassed. As she apologetically explained her situation, my eyes began to well up. It was my turn to dare to be real.

"I know exactly how you feel," I said. "My husband and I were told the same thing, and I had to take those injections for five years. How about for this first one, we do it together? I can give you the shot." We laughed and held hands, and within moments, what had been such a scary undertaking had become a small victory.

That moment was the first *daring to be real* chapter in our book. This wasn't about two people meeting around their strengths; it was about two people letting each other in on their weaknesses. This wasn't Charlotte the speaker preaching and Natalie the singer performing; this was one woman who knew the agony of a dream delayed standing with another in the same seemingly impossible circumstance. Reality is when we peel off the layers we think people expect to see so we can find what we truly need.

When Jesus asked the disciples who they really thought He was, they quoted the views of others. All except Peter.

> When Jesus came to the region of Caesarea Philippi, he asked his disciples, "Who do people say the Son of Man is?"
>
> They replied, "Some say John the Baptist; others say Elijah; and still others, Jeremiah or one of the prophets."
>
> "But what about you?" he asked. "Who do you say I am?"
>
> Simon Peter answered, "You are the Messiah, the Son of the living God."
>
> Jesus replied, "Blessed are you, Simon son of Jonah, for this was not revealed to you by flesh and blood, but by my Father in heaven. And I tell you that you are Peter, and on this rock I will build my church, and the gates of Hades will not overcome it. I will give you the keys of the kingdom of heaven; whatever you bind on earth will be bound in heaven, and whatever you loose on earth will be loosed in heaven" (Matthew 16:13-19).

Peter's answer was very different from that of the other disciples. He saw who Jesus really was, and at his answer, something powerful happened. Jesus spoke over Peter who he really was in Him: a rock, a builder of the future, a powerful leader. When we dare to be real, we gain so much more clarity.

I have met people from all over the world who have presented incredible gifts and talents and amazed me with brilliant wisdom and insight. Yet I have walked away from these encounters with no sense of who they really are, what they love, what they struggle with. I have seen the characters they play without seeing them truly live.

In that moment, on the floor of that changing room—surrounded by outfits Nat had been trying on—we realized that this was a picture of how we wanted our friendship to progress. To leave on the floor the things we had used to cover our vulnerability. To choose to discard any extra baggage that didn't have a place on our journey.

That day, daring to be real in one moment took our friendship to a place where years of pretending never would have brought us.

NOTES FROM NATALIE

Charl and I had to get real with each other for our friendship to grow. She was a Bible teacher from England, and I was a singer and songwriter from the United States. That seemed like enough for a smiley, shiny friendship, only hanging out when we were at the same event. Just like how it is with a lot of other people we encounter in the course of our ministries—without a God-prompt, our relationship could have gone no more than skin deep.

Sometimes we can even try to keep God at this arm's-length level of relationship, but He will not settle for that. He wants to be a Friend and Father to the real *you*. And He already knows who you are! The bits that you like and the bits that maybe you'd like to change—He sees it all, and He is still there.

When I let Charl in on my weakness, on the thing I was struggling with, that's when we started to connect. Often we don't go looking for God's help when we are feeling on top of it all. It's in our weakness that we sense our need for Him.

God wants you to come to Him and have a real conversation, to be free in His presence. On your best day, on your worst day, He wants to hear your voice. He has a plan for you because you are His beautiful and unique creation. When you spend time with Him, that's when He starts to show you the purpose He has marked out for your life.

God promises,

> When you pass through the waters, I will be with you;
>   and when you pass through the rivers,
>   they will not sweep over you.
> When you walk through the fire,
>   you will not be burned;
>   the flames will not set you ablaze (Isaiah 43:2).

We might wish this passage said *if. If* you pass through the waters; *if* you walk through the fire. Unfortunately, the Bible says *when*. Trouble will come— but through it, God will be with us. He is on our side, and He does not lose His patience with us.

God will be with you, the real *you*.

Trying to live a picture-perfect life is so hard. The pressure for perfection exists, and some days it's harder than others to let that go. But when you choose the life God wants you to have, you also choose the freedom Jesus gave you when He died for you.

So choose to be the real *you*, the person God sees. Make this song your prayer today. Use these words to lighten the load and lessen your grip of control, giving Him your devotion instead. Dare to be open to what God has in store for you.

You see the real me
Hiding in my skin, broken from within
Unveil me completely
I'm loosening my grasp
There's no need to mask my frailty
'Cause You see the real me

And You love me just as I am
Wonderful, beautiful is what You see
When You look at me[3]

QUESTIONS FOR DISCUSSION AND REFLECTION

- What layers do you need to remove so you can become the real *you* more and more?

- Where has familiarity prevented you from making new discoveries?

- In what areas of your life has the fear of what people think been responsible for shrinking your view of the future?

_____

_____

_____

_____

_____

_____

_____

_____

4

DARE TO PAUSE

Natalie and I are both committed to communication, so we spend a lot of our time writing. She writes songs; I write messages. And in the writing process, both of us have experienced writer's block. This is a place where you feel stuck. You know more needs to be written, but the words don't seem to flow. They form in your head but don't make enough sense to be committed to the page.

When Nat was writing songs for her album *No Stranger*, she spent 18 months not being able to get the words on paper—words that she felt in her heart but couldn't express in the lyrics of a song.

In such moments, it can be tempting to push through and get some words, *any* words, onto the page. If we found success with our words in the past, does this wordlessness make us failures? In our frustration, we keep wrestling with words that just won't come.

But Nat and I have found that what we force out is what we later discard. Because of the pressure of a deadline, our hands stay busy trying to create content that our hearts don't feel. Whenever we read back over those words, we see that the rhythm changes. Where there had been a flow to the content, now the words are out of step, awkward, and clumsy. The words that pressure produces become superfluous space fillers that ease anxiety for a moment, only to be deleted later.

When I write my books, the delete button is my friend, as it eradicates my "anything will do" pages. However, life is not that simple. We don't have a delete button for the pages stress starts to write. We don't get to erase what we wish we hadn't said. That's why, when we are writing our stories, we must learn to pause. It doesn't seem a big dare to take, and yet when we have a deadline waiting, we rarely consider pausing. To press pause in the place where we feel the pressure to produce seems counterintuitive. Rest is seen as a luxury rather than a necessity. But I have discovered, in life and in writing, to step back and wait. To allow the space I couldn't fill to be a place of stillness.

Over the next few days in England, a friendship between four strangers was about to develop. We didn't have an agenda for what we should be discussing, no big plan for how this chapter should read. No one was striving to control the dialogue, and no one wanted more lines in the script. This chapter could either be forced or find a flow. One option required a lot of expected and controlled conversations, while the other required daring to be comfortable in the *selah*.

SELAH

You may not be familiar with the word *selah*. It's a Hebrew word that we see in some parts of Scripture. It appears to be an instruction for us to pause, to listen, to be still, to quietly think about what was just said. It's written down so that we are reminded not to rush past what we can only discover in the pause.

Selah is the moment that can seem like a much longer passage of time, when everything in you feels it should respond. But *selah* says, "Let it rest; let those words be heard." It's a time to think and to process the important things that, if you hurry, you will miss.

We can see the power of the *selah* in this psalm:

> You, LORD, are a shield around me,
> My glory, and the One who lifts my head.
> I was crying out to the LORD with my voice,
> And He answered me from His holy mountain. *Selah*
> (Psalm 3:3-4 NASB).

Perhaps the psalmist is saying, "Don't just read this truth and carry on." Perhaps he is telling us to pause, to absorb this revelation of the majesty of our God and let it sink in, because pausing in this place will change how we enter the next space.

I think we often fail to see the significance of the *selah* moments, especially when we sense that we are called to be doing something or working on a project. Our need to keep going can mean we miss being fully present in the moments that can maximize and transform our time. When something is new, we tend to think we don't have time to pause—yet I have found the opposite to be true. It's in the early stages of our work that we need more *selah* moments, more places to be still. We need the willingness to stop as much as we need the energy to continue.

I have learned this in my own work. After writing 15 books, I have found a whole new level of appreciation for the gift of an editor, someone who understands that sometimes many words need to become less, and those words that get to stay should then be properly punctuated. This book would not be a blessing to anyone without the skill set of a friend who constantly reminds me of the need for punctuation. The addition of a comma or a period is not meant to stop the flow but to enhance it, to make what I write become something other people can enjoy reading. We need the same commitment on our journey: a commitment to allow the addition of punctuation.

When my fingers are busy getting words on paper, I don't think about how they will eventually read. It takes the eyes of someone who understands the power of the pause, the importance of the paragraph—someone who can take all the words and say, "Now let's add some moments for the reader to reflect." *Selah.*

That's how our story is supposed to read, with the Holy Spirit helping us add the punctuation to our pages. We can rush ahead and carry on, or we can put in a period to finish that sentence strong. Punctuating our lives takes time, attention, and patience—and that's why so often the dare to pause is much greater than we realize.

A pause can feel strange, and the silence it brings can feel uncomfortable. At the start of my friendship with Nat, there were awkward moments when we wondered, *What's this all about? What comes next?* The awkward can start to drive your decisions if you allow its voice to be the loudest, but that's where the *selah* needs to be inserted.

When you go on a first date or interview for a job, the conversation might be tricky. Healthy relationships are ones where you discover a level of ease, where you and your friend or partner are comfortable to talk and also just be. Where you don't have to force a conversation to feel a sense of connection. That comfort in the pause is something that takes time to discover, but once found, *selah* moments allow the flow to replace the forced.

Pausing in this

place will change

how we enter

the next space.

CLUMSY CONVERSATIONS

In 1 Kings, we read how God told the prophet Elijah to go to the "Desert of Damascus" (19:15) and anoint an unsuspecting young man called Elisha. This awkward encounter is one to which I can relate. Their first meeting was not exactly tidy; Scripture records their honest and clumsy conversation.

> Elijah went up to him and threw his cloak around him. Elisha then left his oxen and ran after Elijah. "Let me kiss my father and mother goodbye," he said, "and then I will come with you."
>
> "Go back," Elijah replied. "What have I done to you?" (1 Kings 19:19-20).

Neither Elijah nor Elisha knew how this relationship was going to develop; this was a connection they hadn't envisaged for their future. It was set up by God, and that meant they were starting with a blank page.

The moment the cloak dropped on this young man's shoulders may seem, at first glance, such a powerful and exciting event in Elisha's life. When I read this, though, I feel this was more of an awkward moment than it was anointed. The older prophet asked, "What have I done to you?" while Elisha realized he was going to have to leave his parents. No one was ready for this to happen; it appears the conversation got stuck as neither man quite knew what the best response would be.

Rather than force Elisha's next step, Elijah left a gap. That allowed Elisha to be honest about the things he needed to take care of so that he could join this journey unencumbered by the baggage from his present. Elisha needed the space to process what was coming next. God wants us to add such pauses in our lives too. These are the places where you know you just need to take a breath so you can better find the words for what's ahead.

If we force the next lines, we leave what should have been said unsaid and say too quickly what we don't need to say just yet. Elisha had some goodbyes to make before he was ready to say hello to these new adventures. He had some responsibilities to take care of in order to close the last chapter.

In many ways this was a dare for both of these men, as one was releasing what he felt God had asked him to initiate and the other was releasing what he had always known as his place of belonging and identity. Both needed to dare to pause—and, in that gap, the words were found to close one chapter and start the next.

> Elisha left him and went back. He took his yoke of oxen and slaughtered them. He burned the plowing equipment to cook the meat and gave it to the people, and they ate. Then he set out to follow Elijah and became his servant (1 Kings 19:21).

If we don't allow the blank page to intimidate us, then we can dare to trust the author who placed all the characters in our story. Only God knows their contribution to each chapter. When we force one another to move ahead too quickly, we can end up making people feel pushed into a place they might not want to occupy or don't feel called to fill. In turn, that can lead to resentment as we inadvertently become the enforcer of the story we perceive needs to be told.

Elijah didn't want to be the keeper of Elisha's future, and in Elijah's release, Elisha found his own response. That's why we have to learn to dare to pause, to take a time-out, to allow the awkward silence so that what comes next finds its right level in our lives.

We see another example of this in the book of Ruth, when Naomi was heading back to her homeland after the loss of her husband and sons. Bereaved in the loss of her family and any promise for the future, she began her journey back to Bethlehem, accompanied by her daughters-in-law. But Naomi knew that as much as she would gain comfort from their company, she shouldn't force the story. She was courageous enough to pause and assess the very last relationships she had. It would have been natural to try to control or even manipulate these young women, to encourage them to stay with her and take care of her in her later years. Instead, Naomi created a pause.

> Naomi said to her two daughters-in-law, "Go back, each of you, to your mother's home. May the LORD show you kindness, as you have shown kindness to your dead husbands and to me. May the LORD grant that each of you will find rest in the home of another husband" (Ruth 1:8-9).

Naomi created a pause, allowing her daughters-in-law to go and build a different future if they desired, one that was not attached to her. Orpah chose to return to her family, and Ruth discovered her deep commitment to Naomi.

Sometimes we are too frightened to pause because of what we might lose—but we often forget what we may gain. Elijah gained a committed servant in Elisha who would carry his legacy; Naomi gained a daughter in Ruth who would remain by her side as her own story unfolded in the most beautiful and God-ordained way.

The best connections come when we lessen our control and expectations and instead allow space and time to help develop the conversation. I remember a few days into our time together in England, sitting and listening to the conversation between the four of us. We talked about the highs and lows of our own journeys, and in the many pauses we found God inserting moments that connected our stories, often in the most funny and unexpected ways. Like the moment Nat found out my husband was also a diehard Seattle Seahawks fan as he, too, had grown up in Washington State. You can imagine that got the conversation flowing at a whole new level as countless NFL moments were recounted with so much passion and often a full, dramatic reenactment. Or the moment our husbands realized they had a shared background in classical music education and talked for hours about various musical forms, conductors, and composers.

It was because of the pause that we found a flow that prevented us from trying to control the script. Agendas that could have been awkward were replaced by what could be seen as inconsequential conversations…but that's the thing about pauses. At first glance they don't seem to hold any value; they just serve as space between what appear to be the more essential tasks. Yet when I look back on so much of our journey, I see how daring to pause, being willing not to force connections, allowed room for the very places we found to breathe, to be ourselves. We realized there is time and space for everyone to take a *selah*, to ask, "Do we want to take this next step?" The resistance to rush created the permission to pause.

God doesn't ask us to have robotic, overproduced, and overmanaged lives. He wants us to have relational lives that flow, so that the joy of those unscripted moments becomes the strength for the moments when we feel the text is more testing.

Jesus came and started a flow of conversation with the disciples using the simple words, "Follow Me." Then He left a pause no one knew how to fill. He wanted His followers to know that their discipleship wouldn't be based on a script they had to repeat; it was going to be a flow they would have to find.

Sometimes we overplan the plan. We want every detail filled in, and many times, we don't even realize that a pause could be a part of that plan. Perhaps in your relationships, in your dreams or aspirations, it's time for you to dare to put down the pen and pick up trust. To take a pause, to allow some punctuation in the progress you have been pursuing, to measure the words written under pressure.

Ultimately, we have to come back to the promise we see in this verse:

> "I know the plans I have for you," declares the LORD, "plans to pros-
> per you and not to harm you, plans to give you hope and a future"
> (Jeremiah 29:11).

When we make a plan, it is based on our limited knowledge. Like the time I planned an incredible summer party for all my friends in our yard—but didn't know there was going to be a torrential rainstorm on the exact same day. Or the time I planned a surprise for a friend—but the surprise was that she was not at home when the surprise was delivered. The best plans we can make are based on our limited knowledge, but when the God who knows all and is over all makes plans, they are immune from surprises. If God knows the plan, surely there are times when we need to be okay with not knowing.

Perhaps the areas where we strive the most are the areas where we need to step back and work on our trust in God. Our overworking may mean we are missing the pause in which we would see and hear things that are essential for what comes next. I am so thankful that God puts rest into our journeys, that the Sabbath was built into the whole of creation as part of God's divine strategy. He wants a pause so you can process; He wants a stillness so you can trust His guidance.

God brings us together for His purpose, of that I am sure. But He also brings us together for a pause. This is what makes this journey a joy: the pause that allows the walls to come down so the right words can be found.

The friendship between Nat and me was going to grow and develop, and we would later find that God had a purpose in eventually putting together our ministries. However, as I look back now at these initial meetings, none of that was ever part of the conversation.

The resistance

to rush created

the permission

to pause.

When Nat and Bernie got on a plane and left England, we had no big plan worked out for what came next. We didn't have an amazing idea of how we would achieve something great for God. We hadn't embarked on a fresh journey together with a fixed destination in mind. Yet we parted with a lot of life and heart shared, a lot of laughter and memories made, a deeper appreciation for one another. We had unknowingly taken a week where our dare was to embrace the pause—and later we would find that those moments were crucial. The flow we had found was going to be the vehicle that, much later, would be used to solidify the foundation for our ministry.

NOTES FROM NATALIE

This journey we went on as two friends would eventually mean adding many more commitments to our already busy lives. But God wasn't trying to make us work harder for Him; He just wanted to teach us how to work alongside Him. Finding the rhythm of His grace includes discovering these *selah* moments.

As a songwriter, I am so familiar with the beauty of this pause; *selah* is a musical term found many times in the book of Psalms and a few times in Habakkuk. *Selah* fuels me for the things I am called to do. It's the pause I sometimes don't even know I need, the time to reconnect with the flow I have somehow lost.

We all feel exhausted at times. We feel like we're always running until we're running on empty. Sometimes our faith can seem so vibrant and alive, and sometimes it can seem dead, or God can feel distant. I used to be ashamed to admit that, because it made me feel like I was a bad Christian. But then I realized we all have these moments. It has nothing to do with the Lord; it has everything to do with our humanity.

My song "Face to Face" is an exploration of the times when my well has run dry and I have had to take myself back to the source to fill up again. When I am tired, when I feel I can't put one foot in front of the other, I have learned to remind myself, *I have known His goodness; I have known His faithfulness.* When I am dry, He fills me and picks me up again. God always sees, always knows, and nothing takes Him by surprise.

One of my favorite scriptures is Psalm 91—it's the 911 of my spiritual life!

> Those who live in the shelter of the Most High
> will find rest in the shadow of the Almighty (Psalm 91:1 NLT).

This promise is for those who make the Lord their dwelling every day, in the good and the bad. When we build our life on His truth, even on those days when we struggle to believe it, we can hold on to the promise that His truth never fails. We need to be those who set up camp in His presence. We need to declare that, whatever happens, we are not moving out.

> This I declare about the LORD:
> He alone is my refuge, my place of safety;
>   he is my God, and I trust him.
> For he will rescue you from every trap
>   and protect you from deadly disease (Psalm 91:2-3 NLT).

Even when we feel far, God comes close. You know that safety and security you experience when you hold the hand of someone you love? That's the feeling we can have when we're with the Lord. Whatever is raging around us, we can experience the safety and security that only comes when we're standing hand in hand with the Lord.

So if you are feeling downcast and your spirit is overwhelmed, run to Him, stay there, live in His presence. Trust Him for the uncertain times ahead, find rest in the *selah* of His shadow—and in so doing, you will find the strength to soar again.

Dare to pause in God's presence today. Dare to stop filling the gaps with words that are not needed and, instead, just breathe. Take the time to focus on His Word and who He is. Reach out for a moment and devote some time to being in an attitude of worship. Take hold of the hand He is extending toward you today and use the words of this song as your prayer.

My eyes have seen Your hand deliver
My heart remembers You, my help and my defender
My well runs dry, but I've known the taste of rain
So I'll wait, I'll wait for You

Here I am, I'm reachin' out
I need You always, oh, I need You now
I'm comin' close so we can stay
Hand in hand until we stand face to face

I still believe in new beginnings
The battle rages, but I still believe You'll win it
The night will bend to the light that's breakin' through
So I'll wait, I'll wait for You[4]

QUESTIONS FOR DISCUSSION AND REFLECTION

- In what ways have you noticed that you need to press *pause* in your life?

- What part of your life needs some punctuation?

- What tangible steps can you take to add some stillness to your story?

5

DARE TO BEGIN

After a few days of getting to know our new friends, it was time for them to fly home. I remember thinking, *Well, that was great*, but also feeling unsure about what would come next. We knew God's fingerprints were all over what was happening, but we sensed that it was now up to us to figure out how to follow.

It's like when you enter the coordinates to a new destination into your GPS. At the start there are lots of instructions—*turn left, turn right*. You get comfortable and trust the voice, as the device clearly knows where you are going.

Then there's that stretch of road with no instructions and you wonder, *Did the GPS lose connection? Am I heading in the wrong direction?* The reality is, you're just going to spend a while on this road before you need a new instruction. This part of the journey requires you to follow the path you're already on. Similarly, we believed God had launched us on the journey with such a miraculous set of instructions, and now that we were on the right road, He was going to let us figure some things out on our own.

We want clear instructions every step of the way, but God is our Father. When you think about the relationship in those terms, you realize that being a good father means allowing moments in the children's lives when they move from simply following instructions to taking some steps for themselves. I remember when I taught my children to ride a bike; they went from the safety of training wheels to removing them and having me run alongside the bicycle, holding them steady and giving them lots of encouragement. Then there was the moment when I knew they had enough momentum and instruction that I could let go and they would pedal all by themselves.

God is a good Father, and He can add training wheels to our lives for a season when we are about to embark on a new adventure. He can also remove those wheels when it's the right time, so we don't become so reliant on an outside sign that we lose the ability to trust that inner voice.

There is a point in all our journeys when we need to allow the training wheels to come off. When Esther told her cousin Mordecai that she couldn't do anything to help her people, his response seemed almost shocking—but he had nurtured and cared for her, and he knew it was time for her to step up and put his teachings into practice.

> When Esther's words were reported to Mordecai, he sent back this answer: "Do not think that because you are in the king's house you alone of all the Jews will escape. For if you remain silent at this time, relief and deliverance for the Jews will arise from another place, but you and your father's family will perish. And who knows but that you have come to your royal position for such a time as this?" (Esther 4:12-14).

In a sense, Mordecai was letting Esther know, "I have brought you this far, and now it's your turn." Esther had been following the lead, but it was time for her to become the leader. She had to begin a conversation with the king, and no one else was going to write the script for her.

Esther knew she was risking her life in even approaching the king. "I will go to the king, even though it is against the law," she said. "And if I perish, I perish" (Esther 4:16).

When we don't make the shift from follower to leader, we can depend too much on the voices and support systems around us. We can become so comfortable in our supporting role that we fail to recognize when the script requires something more from us. When we become over-reliant on external factors, we can slow our own progress. If we always need the big word, the orange-sweater moment, we can move from being obedient to being high maintenance. Nat and I definitely needed that God-intervention to get us on the same page, in the same nation at the same time, but now I was sensing we needed to be willing to trust the Holy Spirit's nudge and dare to accelerate along a road not as clearly marked.

Let's be honest, long-distance relationships are not easy to navigate, and with our training wheels removed, Nat and I would both have to pedal. To start, we only needed to use a middle gear for a smooth ride, but as the landscape shifted, we needed to apply more pedal power and move through the lower gears. God in His kindness doesn't move us faster than He knows we can handle with His help, but He also knows when it's time for the incline or when we need that downhill boost of adrenaline. Nat and I were about to increase our spiritual muscles by pedaling over some new terrain.

For the first couple years we learned to pedal as friends, and as we leaned into the relationship, we found there was a beautiful ease and grace in our flourishing friendship. We were real friends; we shared openly and talked at length about all the things that concerned and challenged us, blessed and excited us. We had taken our time to pedal at a pace that allowed a strong foundation to

form. We celebrated moments and made memories with birthdays and anniversaries spent together—our wedding anniversaries are only a day apart! We even went on vacations together, and we all know that's where you really find out if a friendship can survive.

As we spoke, we sometimes shared what we were working on, and we found that so often God was speaking to us from the exact same place in Scripture. Nat would share about the song she was writing, or I would talk about a message I was creating, and we would find that we were both inspired by the same thought or emphasis.

I remember one day I was in Nat's home, which had become my home base every time I was stateside. I was there for a few days while I was writing my book *The Miracle in the Middle*. On that particular day, I was sitting at her dining room table and writing about how it's only in the middle of the storm that you see the water-walking Jesus. I was typing away when Nat came up from the studio where she had been recording. "Hey," she said, "want to come hear this new song? It's about that storm where the disciples are in the boat and Jesus spoke to them on the water."

As I entered the studio, she began to play the song "Hurricane." I sat and listened and began to cry as I said, "Let me read you what I'm writing." Our words had been written in different spaces but were on the exact same page.

CHANGING TERRAIN

We were fast becoming each other's biggest cheerleaders, yet I have discovered that God rarely goes to all that trouble just to help a few; it's always with a purpose that will bless many. And so, looking back, perhaps it's not a surprise that we both felt stirred spiritually, believing that God was asking us to begin a ministry. We certainly didn't plan this, but now every conversation seemed to be pointing in that direction. We sensed that God had a purpose for us to go and help others. We felt that if *we* needed each other, there were many more who also needed to find a place of connection and friendship, a place where they could hear God speak into their story.

The terrain was changing, and this would require a new willingness to shift gears together. It was time for something new to begin; God was asking us to apply our gifts and talents to the terrain in front of us. But it made no sense to consider doing ministry together—how could we combine our different gifts when we both had young children and lived an ocean apart?

After a God-ordained beginning, faith has to find expression in deeds. This is when the action starts to happen—and costs start to be incurred. Up until now the investment had been in a friendship, but now we were talking about investing in a ministry. With any new beginning comes a whole list of requests and demands. We were aware that to begin would also mean to invest, and we had no idea of the cost. That's when we found ourselves in this passage of Scripture:

> Suppose one of you wants to build a tower. Won't you first sit down
> and estimate the cost to see if you have enough money to complete
> it? (Luke 14:28).

I meet a lot of people who have a dream but no plan to take care of the implications of that dream. They talk about the God-idea as if it's God's bill to pay. While I do believe God always helps supply seed to the sower and provision for the vision, I also know He wants us to apply our skills, to use our God-given abilities, and to be good stewards financially.

As we both counted the cost, we were unsure if we were brave enough to dare to begin; the truth was, we seemed to have more to lose than to gain. We didn't need any of this for our individual ministries; they were already up and running. We didn't need another event, as we both had schedules filled with events. We had a friendship that flourished because it wasn't based around work—this would mean a shift in our relationship too.

We decided to share our idea with others. One thing I have discovered about beginnings is that they need oxygen to breathe, to live. It's easy just to think about it—all good ideas stay as good intentions when all we do is think about them. Once we speak about them, we begin to develop a real attachment.

Our conversations moved from being just between the two of us, to being with our families and then with a team of people who could potentially jump on board with us. I remember sitting at Nat's dining table once again as we both started sharing our deep sense of commitment about leading together through worship and the Word, reaching women with songs and messages of hope. We spoke about how we could help women of all ages come together to talk about real life as we got real with them. As we spoke, we could sense that momentum was gaining.

It was at that table that someone asked the question, "Well, what would you call this?" We all sat quietly and thought about it, and then someone said, "Well, you are going to have to really step out and dare to do this." And we realized that's exactly what this was—it was daring to begin, daring to believe, and daring to *be*. That day, at that table, Dare to Be was born. The ministry we had been incubating now had a name, so now we had to dare to create it.

At the beginning of anything new, the enemy responds with his offensive plan. He wants the idea never to get out of the starting block; he wants you to be defeated by doubts and overwhelmed by obstacles. He wants to stop what you are carrying from ever developing because it's much easier to defeat what hasn't even found its feet. Consider that when Moses was born, there was an edict in the land that all baby boys were to be killed at birth. Before the life of Moses could even begin, there was already a plan in place to eradicate him.

> Pharaoh gave this order to all his people: "Every Hebrew boy that
> is born you must throw into the Nile, but let every girl live" (Exo-
> dus 1:22).

It was only because of God's provision that Moses was able to live to change history.

Later we see an attack to shut down another part of the story as we read about the expedition into the promised land, which was tainted by the negative report that overwhelmed the voices of Joshua and Caleb.

> The men who had gone up with him [Caleb] said, "We can't attack
> those people; they are stronger than we are." And they spread among
> the Israelites a bad report about the land they had explored (Num-
> bers 13:31-32).

Joshua and Caleb dared to begin what God had already promised was ahead for them, but fear and negativity caused the plan to be aborted, and the destiny of a whole generation was stalled.

We can also look at the example of Jesus' life. After His birth He was sought out by Herod, who wanted to kill Him (Matthew 2:13-18).

Beginnings are often battlegrounds where you have to dare to push past what would otherwise shut you down. That's exactly what we were about to experience just a few months after that meeting where we named our new beginning "Dare to Be." Little did we know what would follow. Perhaps that's why God doesn't show us too much up front; we likely wouldn't commit if we knew all the hidden costs.

At first we gained a lot of traction; the excitement of this new idea was helping us dream big and begin. We went ahead and planned our first tour.

Let me stop here for a moment. Touring was something I had never even considered, and when Nat suggested we get on a tour bus and travel across the United States with a band and a tech team, I said, "Well, maybe I can just fly and meet you at the next city." The idea of living and sleeping on a bus, being in my pj's with the tour group members—whom I had never met before—was already making me rethink this idea. Nat assured me this was the best way to do the tour and so, not fully convinced myself, a plan was put in motion.

Then came the obstacles, which I now see as tests we needed to pass in order for this idea to live. Nat and I were definitely taking this dare personally, as this project was going to be funded by our own budgets. We had faith for provision, and we had hope that we would see people show up in the venues we had booked for the event.

When we arrived at the first venue, a bead curtain—in theory a great prop for making the stage look glamorous on a tight budget—came out of the trailer a tangled and knotted mess that seemed impossible to unravel. For that first event, we didn't even get to our rehearsal—Nat and I spent the afternoon untangling the beads as the crew set up. That was when we started saying our now much-loved expression: "Yay for me, I'm daring to be!" (Or "bead," as it were.)

That first tour was already off to a difficult start—but then it got worse. A tornado swept through a town where we were heading, and the only building that took irreparable damage was the one we had booked for our event. Then there was the break-in at the place where our brand-new database was installed; the one computer that went missing was the one with all the information we needed and had spent weeks gathering. Then our children got incredibly sick, out of nowhere. Oh, and a snake attack. Yep, you read that right—a huge rattlesnake sprang at my husband. Fortunately he was with the guy who came to remove it and didn't get hurt.

I am sure when Noah began building the ark, he didn't say on day one (or even year one), "Wow, look how awesome this is!" I am sure on day one of rebuilding the walls of Jerusalem, Nehemiah didn't think, *Well, that was easy.* On day one of being a disciple of Jesus, I'm sure neither Peter nor Andrew nor John nor James nor any of the others walked away thinking, *Yeah, I get this new way of living. I understand this new teaching.*

Beginnings are not for the fainthearted. The enemy is invested in sabotaging beginnings because he knows that once God gets something off the starting block, things begin to change. He knew that after the ark was constructed, the flood would arrive. He knew that after Moses was born and taken in by Pharaoh's daughter, the deliverance of God's people was inevitable. He knew that after the walls of Jerusalem were rebuilt, the people would gather and worship again. He knew that after Jesus arrived, death would be conquered.

When you face obstacles at the beginning, you have to remind yourself of the reason for the opposition. Nothing good begins without someone, somewhere, taking a dare. For Nat and I as friends, the beginning was testing, but it was also defining. We had to keep coming back to that place of commitment. Our prayer life grew, our belief went deeper, and we realized we could shift to a whole other gear. We'd dared to begin, and now we were about to discover a new momentum.

NOTES FROM NATALIE

In the moment when the storm rages, when the obstacles are all we can see, each of us responds differently. Charl and I navigated these storms together, finding our way back to the One who is the constant in every situation—finding a way to worship when the waves were raging.

On this journey we have had to stand strong in many different storms. Charl mentioned that we both had to face the storm of infertility. It's something I had to learn to navigate, and it was no overnight miracle. There were times when my husband and I questioned the journey we were on. But so often God gives us more than we expect, just not at the time we expect it. So when I eventually got pregnant, there were two heartbeats: Bella and Gracie. Fast-forward almost four years after their arrival, and we were blessed with Sadie too. So today, by God's grace, I am a mother of three.

Sounds perfect, right? Well, as Charl mentioned, we both wrote on the same theme at the same time; the song "Hurricane" was my way of calling out to God through the storm of postpartum depression. I felt so ashamed about suffering from depression; the guilt was overwhelming. I felt like such a bad Christian, a failure both privately and publicly. How could I write songs in the hope of healing others in their depression but struggle to apply the truths of these songs to my own life? I felt like a fraud. The lights had been turned off in my life, and I didn't know how I was going to find a way back.

Eventually, I got the help I needed to step out from the shame. I was learning to be transparent. There is no denying these times in life are tough; it's so much easier when we are on the mountain with the Lord. That's where the disciples were before the storm in Matthew 14. They were with Jesus, seeing incredible miracles take place. Who knew a storm was coming?

> Immediately Jesus made the disciples get into the boat and go on ahead of him to the other side, while he dismissed the crowd. After he had dismissed them, he went up on a mountainside by himself to pray. Later that night, he was there alone, and the boat was already a considerable distance from land, buffeted by the waves because the wind was against it (Matthew 14:22-24).

We learn more about God's character in the storm than on the mountain. In this passage we see that Jesus insisted the disciples go on ahead of Him. He knew the storm was coming, and He sent them into its path all the same. When the storm was raging, that's when Jesus appeared to them—He had come down off the mountain and was right there in the storm with them.

> Shortly before dawn Jesus went out to them, walking on the lake. When the disciples saw him walking on the lake, they were terrified. "It's a ghost," they said, and cried out in fear.
>
> But Jesus immediately said to them: "Take courage! It is I. Don't be afraid."
>
> "Lord, if it's you," Peter replied, "tell me to come to you on the water."
>
> "Come," he said (Matthew 14:25-29).

Peter responded differently from the other disciples; he didn't want to wait for the waves to die down. It would have been easier to stay in the boat until the storm had passed, but he set off anyway. Like Peter, we have to believe God has already done His work. He is there with us, and we can grab hold of the hand of mercy He's extending.

So friend, don't hide away. Reach out for God's hand and dare to begin with us. As we close this chapter, I want to remind you of the words of the song "Hurricane," because maybe the words I wrote in my storm can help you in yours. Don't let the storm be your ending, but rather your new beginning. Worship these words into your life.

Step out on the edge
Don't be afraid of it
And when you feel the rain
Call His name
He'll find you in the hurricane

Don't back down from the fight
He'll shelter you tonight
Just hold on for the change
Call His name
He'll find you in the hurricane[5]

QUESTIONS FOR DISCUSSION AND REFLECTION

- What is it time to begin?

- What investment might you need to make to build the future you want?

- What obstacle are you currently facing that could become an opportunity?

6

DARE TO BUILD

I mentioned in the last chapter that before I met Natalie, I had no idea what tour life was like. The bus accommodation situation was all new to me. I was living out of a small suitcase, going to sleep in a bus bunk in one city and then waking up in the next city. At times I forgot I was sleeping in a bunk and gave myself a mild concussion trying to get up in the middle of the night. I would also forget that the place in which I was walking was also moving. I discovered that the sound of the bus on the road is like white noise, which is helpful when your bus buddy in the bunk across from you likes to sleep with the sound of white noise. As friends Nat and I were bonding on all levels; we had moved from dreaming to literally getting on the road.

Daring to be means experiencing discomfort. It means stretching—but also being strengthened. Our bus-life diaries were being written, and they were pretty amusing. I remember one day, about a week into our tour, strolling off the bus around midday and going to a hotel to check in so I could take a shower. As I stood there in the hotel lobby, asking for the room key, I wondered why people were staring at me. I took a look at myself and realized I was in my pj's, like it was normal attire in a public place. That's when I knew the bus experience had taken over my life just a little too much.

It's amazing what we think we can't do until we begin to do it, what we say will never work until it's actually working. Beginnings get us rolling, but it's what we build that keeps us growing. We had been given that push to begin, we had persevered past the obstacles to get started, and now it was time to build.

As we started touring, we were aware that the decisions we were making then would determine what we would build for the future. As individuals, Nat and I had spent many years building our lives and ministries. People knew what to expect when they heard Natalie's name; she had built a ministry where her music was known and loved. Likewise, I had established my teaching gift, and people who invited me into their churches and events did so because they knew my preaching would deliver what they had come to expect from me. However, when it came to Dare to Be, people really had no idea what to expect. Many knew of Nat, others knew of my teaching, but no one knew what this combination would look like.

Establishing foundations takes time, and we had invested a lot of energy into ours. Yet the thing about foundations is that no one sees them; we all need them, but they are the groundwork established without an audience. No one watches the foundations being laid—but once it gets to building, a very different challenge arises. What we assemble on those foundations is very visible.

Building can be extremely personal. You only have to drive to different areas of your city and look at the architecture to see that each builder had a vision, which is reflected in each building—from the small and minimalist office space to the imposing and stately hotel next to it. Both of those buildings reflect the architects' plans and visions. However, if you were able to see their foundations, they would look similar. It's what has been built above ground level that looks different and individual.

In certain neighborhoods, every house is styled the same, down to the window trim and paint colors. We must be careful when we dare to build that our work doesn't become more copying than creating. The safety net of following what we have always known and are so familiar with can become our blueprint; instead, we should be willing to trust God and build something more bespoke. If we serve a Creator God, then we have to ask ourselves, *Am I allowing the Creator who is within me to guide what I am building?*

As we began to build our new ministry, Nat and I were aware that what was easiest might not be what was best. What could save us time because an architectural plan already existed might not be what we should be building. Listening to those who were cheering us on and those who were urging caution created conflicting versions of what this new thing should look and sound like.

Within weeks of our first tour being established, I remember having many conversations with people who wanted to help us build. These suggestions came from people who wanted to offer their expertise and make this project more successful. They recommended ways to maximize the opportunity before us by allowing them to shape large parts of what we were trying to build.

Although their willingness to help was greatly appreciated, and we were certain their assistance would help alleviate our burden, we had this feeling that God was not asking us to subcontract this project or to follow someone else's plan. Instead, we sensed we should trust Him and dare to build something unique. If we took up all those suggestions and offers of help, we would be moving away from daring to build something new and choosing instead to settle for a prefabricated home.

The temptation was very real. Remember, Nat and I lived an ocean apart, and this was a project for which we hadn't fully scheduled or budgeted. The offer to have someone else build for us, to do the legwork while we went about our regular lives, could have felt like a godsend—had we not had a conviction that this ministry was ours to build. We determined that we weren't going to take the simplest, easiest option in front of us. Let me tell you, that decision was not made lightly by either of us.

Alongside the offers of help in the early stages of building, we also received some rejections when encouragement was really needed, a withholding of help from those who we thought would be cheering us along. I found it hard to accept responses that were less encouraging and supportive than those we were receiving from people we barely knew. I discovered that the thing we were building was seen by some as competition rather than something to celebrate.

To be honest, this caused me to have a wobble and go back to God about what we had committed to build for Him. That's when I had to realize all over again that God had asked *us* to build—and that means everyone else didn't get the memo. Sometimes people won't give planning permission for something God has already granted—and that's why you have to decide who is in charge of your building site. That's when the dare becomes real. When the people you love and look to for support don't show up to cheer you on, you have to trust the One whose idea it was in the first place.

My husband and I recently decided to build an extension on our home—to take the house we had and make it more fitting for our family's needs. This reminded me again of exactly why we often settle for what we know or what we have always seen. The upheaval that decision made in our home and lives was costly and time consuming, but as I write, I'm sitting in a room filled with light that didn't exist a few years ago. That space wasn't in the original design, and now our house doesn't look like the other houses in our neighborhood. It doesn't fit in like it did before, but it fits our family better than it ever has.

When we were working on our house extension, one of our very sweet neighbors had an issue with what we had decided to build. Our burst of creativity was clearly causing a sense of discomfort in our neighborhood. Yet just a short time later, the place that was opposed became a space our neighbors enjoyed. The change may have caused a conflict at first, but it was not long before that resistance became appreciation and our choice became an inspiration to our neighbors, who decided they wanted to expand their homes too. Sometimes it's the bravery of the one who breaks the barrier and builds something new that brings freedom for so many others.

Daring to build means being willing to let go of what has always been for what—without daring—may never be. David dared to build in a way that hadn't been seen before. Imagine if he had remained in the safety of what King Saul had established. He could have chosen to wear the armor and fit the mold when he went out to face Goliath (1 Samuel 17:38-40). But David built a different legacy then and after because he dared to carry on even in the moments when he felt he had to do it alone.

The resistance I received from those who I thought would bring support was either an invitation to stop the building work or an opportunity to develop new skills.

Nat and I were embarking on a journey that was placing us both back on the building site in a way that made us a little uncomfortable. At the same time, though, we could see something beautiful emerging. We felt like we were putting down our microphones and picking up hammers and nails. We were stepping away from our platform and getting our hands dirty. You know you are building something when your thoughts change from *What am I wearing to the event?* to *How am I going to pay the team?* We had conversations about everything from lighting rigs to venue capacities. We had a vision in our hearts of what we wanted, and now we were building the vessel on which it could set sail.

I have found that the vision is rarely the problem. I meet a lot of people who have dreams and ideas, and yet a vision without a vessel diminishes the possibilities. We can talk about our vision. We can read about it and download podcasts about it. But if we are not building vessels to carry it and make it happen, it will just remain a dream.

A little more than a hundred years ago, the dockyards in England were centers of industry. Huge vessels were built there to carry products and passengers across oceans to places that were previously unreachable. The vessels allowed commerce to increase and productivity to be maximized; they allowed possibilities to become realities. In the same way, each dream you have requires you to spend time doing hard work in the dockyard. It's not a glamorous place—but that's where the vision finds the vessel.

An account in 1 Samuel tells of a time when Israel found the enemy advancing against them, and they had no weapons with which to fight them. The Philistines had hatched a plan to remove every possible weapon maker from the people of Israel.

> Not a blacksmith could be found in the whole land of Israel, because the Philistines had said, "Otherwise the Hebrews will make swords or spears!" So all Israel went down to the Philistines to have their plow points, mattocks, axes and sickles sharpened…
>
> So on the day of the battle not a soldier with Saul and Jonathan had a sword or spear in his hand; only Saul and his son Jonathan had them (1 Samuel 13:19-20,22).

The enemy doesn't mind your having a dream; he is not threatened by your big ideas. His plan is not that subtle. He wants you to be so enamored with the vision that you forget to craft the vessel and forge the weapons. He wants to remove from the building site the tools you require to make the dream a reality so that when you face a problem in the construction process, you won't be able to carry on. When you face spiritual attack, you will be missing the weapons with which to fight back.

Nat and I had a dream, but it was only when we were well and truly at work in the dockyard that we discovered we needed to forge some weapons for what was ahead. One of the vessels we needed to build was a way to get people who came to our event to have a personal encounter with Jesus. We sat and talked about our desire to see people saved; we didn't want anyone to leave without an opportunity to find Christ for themselves.

We had a vision to reach people, and we needed a vessel to ensure that could happen, so we planned to build time into every event to do an altar call. We wanted an old-school "If you need Jesus, walk down the aisle and come to the front" moment.

When we first added this to the evening, we sensed a spiritual battle, even to the point where one church venue refused to have the altar call be part of the night. This led to us changing our venue at the last minute and incurring the cost of that decision because we were committed to providing this opportunity to find Jesus.

The enemy is not going to let you build without a fight. We had a vision, and we needed that vessel to be ready. We had to forge in prayer and faith the weapons to fight for people's salvation, to seek God for hearts to be opened. That battle was one we were not willing to quit.

The first night we gave the altar call, I didn't want to open my eyes. What if nobody responded? What if this was too up front? That moment felt like hours, but as I heard Natalie's sniffles behind me, I realized something was happening. The vessel was being boarded by people in the room who wanted to find a way home to their Savior.

Thousands of people have now walked down the aisles at Dare to Be events, from an 85-year-old grandmother to a 13-year-old young lady. One night there were three generations from one family—grandma, daughter, and granddaughter—who walked to the front together, coming to kneel at the altar, ready to surrender to Jesus.

That's why we build. That's why we need to dare to move from the dream to the dockyard. People are waiting for the vessels we are supposed to be building. We need to know how to build with the tools of intercessory prayer and the Word of God in times of fear. We need to know how to worship through the pain, to pray until the breakthrough comes. We need to know how to sow in a time of famine and believe God for a miracle.

Noah's backyard became the original dockyard where he was given a vision that would literally require a big, never-before-seen vessel. Noah had no idea what a worldwide flood would be like; he had no idea what God was really asking of him. And yet the Bible records, "Noah did everything just as God commanded him" (Genesis 6:22).

Bible scholars calculate that it likely took Noah between 55 and 100 years to build the ark. He couldn't give it a month and then ask for another calling. Year in and year out, he had to keep picking up where he left off. It must have been years before he saw any progress. Yet he took responsibility for the work required to build the vessel God had called him to build. His job was to build and then trust God with what would follow.

This passage has always been a challenge to me:

> In a large house there are not only vessels *and* objects of gold and silver, but also vessels *and* objects of wood and of earthenware, and some are for honorable (noble, good) use and some for dishonorable (ignoble, common). Therefore, if anyone cleanses himself from these *things* [which are dishonorable—disobedient, sinful], he

will be a vessel for honor, sanctified [set apart for a special purpose and], useful to the Master, prepared for every good work (2 Timothy 2:20-21 AMP).

We get to decide just how useful our vessel will be. We can settle for a life that has only one use, or we can commit to the journey of removing things from our life that hinder—and of building and investing in the work that will make our vessel more valuable in God's hands. When we dare to build, that process will often begin within our own life. We are called to be a vessel that won't sink in the storm or capsize when opposition increases.

Nat and I were daring to build something we sensed would look different from the work we had done before. Something that would require our time and investment in new ways. We knew this building process wouldn't last for just a few weeks—in fact, we are still building 15 years later. Daring to build begins when we, like Noah, get up and say, "Today is as good a day as any to get to work." And it is work. But let me encourage you: It's good, life-changing work.

Don't settle for cookie cutters when you have the Creator of the universe inside you. Dare to build something that will last, something that isn't on shifting sands. Dare to build, and you will find the process builds something new within you.

NOTES FROM NATALIE

When we build something for God, we will face challenges. I wrote the lyrics of "My Weapon" based on the prayer of Moses in Exodus 33, when he was trying to get the children of Israel to the promised land. They were running wild, ignoring the commandments etched by the hand of God and worshipping a

Dare to build,

and you will

find the process

builds something

new within you.

golden calf. So God took a step back from them. He didn't leave them all alone, but He pulled back His presence.

> The LORD said to Moses, "Leave this place, you and the people you brought up out of Egypt, and go up to the land I promised on oath to Abraham, Isaac and Jacob, saying, 'I will give it to your descendants.' I will send an angel before you and drive out the Canaanites, Amorites, Hittites, Perizzites, Hivites and Jebusites. Go up to the land flowing with milk and honey. But I will not go with you, because you are a stiff-necked people and I might destroy you on the way" (Exodus 33:1-3).

God basically said, "I'm still going to make good on My word to you. I'm still going to deliver you to the promised land, and I'm still with you. I'm just not with you as closely as I was." Moses' reply to the Lord Almighty has become the prayer of my life: *Show me Your glorious presence, Lord.*

> Moses said to him, "If your Presence does not go with us, do not send us up from here. How will anyone know that you are pleased with me and with your people unless you go with us? What else will distinguish me and your people from all the other people on the face of the earth?"
>
> And the LORD said to Moses, "I will do the very thing you have asked, because I am pleased with you and I know you by name."
>
> Then Moses said, "Now show me your glory" (Exodus 33:15-18).

We can be desperate to get to the promised land, but what good is it without God? Dare to Be is not a destination; it's a journey of obedience. God's presence is the prize.

When God shows us His presence, we flourish. Charl and I didn't flourish because Dare to Be started to succeed; we flourished because of obedience. We flourished because we relied on the presence of God to fight against fear and failure, to fight against all the obstacles we had to overcome and are still overcoming. This journey built something within us—a determination and tenacity that deepened the more we realized just how much God was with us and for us.

Dare to build a vehicle to carry others to Jesus. Dare to build a vessel that can be filled with His presence. Today, remind yourself that you have the weapons you need: weapons of prayer and devotion, faith and worship. Take the next few moments and commit to make God's presence your only goal. Speak these words over your life and find true freedom, knowing God goes with you to fight your battles so you can build your vessels.

Let every lie be silenced and all depression cease
Let every dark assignment bow down at Jesus' feet
Let every curse be broken, let every storm be tamed
And all that come against us be bound in Jesus' name

Your presence is my greatest weapon
Pushing back the darkness, breaking every chain
My worship opens up the heavens
Crushing every stronghold when I speak Your name
'Cause Your presence is my weapon
Your presence is my weapon[6]

QUESTIONS FOR DISCUSSION AND REFLECTION

- In what way does your dream need to go to the dockyard?

- What part of your story do you need to get involved in again?

- What steps will you take to put that part of your life back under construction?

7

DARE TO FAIL

nyone who has ever built anything knows that the process rarely goes according to plan. Part of daring to build is daring to fail. It all sounds perfect when it's just on paper, but in practice, things are different. That may be why we don't want to dare to build—because we don't want to risk failing. The building process will test your patience, your peace, and your relationships.

That was something Nat and I were discovering on our journey. We had a great friendship, but now we were becoming coworkers and fellow business owners. That was moving our relationship into brand-new territory, and we soon realized that if our friendship was going to survive this stage of building, then we had to become comfortable with failing.

No one sets out wanting to fail, but I also believe no one really wins without learning how to fail well. David, Moses, and Peter all failed—need I go on? The heroes of our faith were people who dared to fail.

Failure is something we would rather gloss over; we rarely post about it or take a selfie in the midst of it. But when we acknowledge failure, we deny its power. When we admit how far we've fallen, we can learn from the experience and teach others in turn.

Nat and I had to allow each other a place to fail; we needed to recognize that there was enough space for both of us to make a bad call. We had to be open to hard conversations when we felt we might have let the other person down.

It's probably worth mentioning at this point that the two of us have very different personalities. Nat has tremendous drive and strength, and I'm more comfortable being a helper, coming alongside others. This is a combination that can work well, as each strength supports the other's weakness—but our differences can also mean that when something goes wrong, we both react in opposite ways. Nat is the one who tackles a problem head-on, and she can quickly forgive and move forward. I tend to take a problem on board and then keep carrying it, and I make things more personal than they should be. I can find it hard to move forward, needing to know everyone is happy first; Nat knows that everyone being happy is a good goal but not always the right one.

So here we were building a ministry together, learning how to put our gifts to work side by side, something that takes time and intention. This wasn't about sharing a platform; it was about sharing a life and calling. I had to deal with some insecurities that were now staring me in the face. Onstage I felt inadequate—I mean, who wants to follow Nat's incredible voice? She was always so encouraging and never made me feel like I didn't measure up, but I had some idea in my mind of what I needed to bring to the table, and I felt like I was failing.

When we allow insecurity into our headspace, it changes everything we see and hear. I was new to the world of touring, and I was very aware of the mistakes I was making—from learning how team dynamics worked within a band that had been together for years, to navigating the temptation to be someone God hadn't made me to be.

Nat and I held Q and A sessions every night before each event, and after about a week of doing these, I felt like I was lacking. It was obvious that the attendees had been listening to Nat's music for years, and they really just wanted to ask about her songwriting and grab a picture with her. I started feeling like I was holding her back. People came to the event to hear her sing, and every night Nat would say, "Hey, if you're expecting a concert, get ready for something very different." I worried that the crowd would be disappointed. They were up for the singing, but would they want to hear preaching?

But here's the thing: I was only failing in my own mind. I had created a hurdle that no one else was asking me to jump, and I was stuck thinking I wasn't contributing enough to the team. It took a lot of honest conversations and some tears to help me see that I wasn't failing in my work—but I *was* failing in my thoughts.

Failure isn't always visible; it can be an area in our mind that we allow to become a brake to our future. Consider Gideon, who viewed himself as the weakest of the weak.

> "Pardon me, my lord," Gideon replied, "but how can I save Israel? My clan is the weakest in Manasseh, and I am the least in my family" (Judges 6.15).

Those words were his admission that he was failing and that he came from a family of failures. But God had sent a word to Gideon that focused on what he had already been given.

> The Lord turned to him and said, "Go in the strength you have and save Israel out of Midian's hand. Am I not sending you?" (verse 14).

The weakness was not the failure; the failure was ignoring the strength he already had. That's what I needed to be reminded of, and it took a patient and

You can choose

to let failure

define you or

refine you.

strong friend to speak those same words over me. You can choose to let failure define you or refine you.

Besides the personal feelings of failing, Nat and I also had those moments when what we wanted to see happen was not what we were experiencing. When we were just starting to build the ministry of Dare to Be, we were going to all kinds of venues, some in places neither of us had ever been to before. We hoped to reach new people in those communities. In one such location, it was only a week or so out from the event when we realized that the venue size and the ticket sales were not matching up. That was when we both had to face what we perceived as failure in a way that taught us a valuable lesson.

At the start of both our ministries, we had known how it felt to preach or sing to an audience of one—plus a few family members we had asked to fill the seats. As life moved on and our individual ministries gained momentum, it was easy to forget that early stage. We had grown comfortable with a room full of people hungry to hear and be a part of what we were doing. So on this particular evening, we both felt discomfort and disappointment as we faced a room that was less than half full and an audience not fully convinced they were going to like what we had to offer.

From backstage we peeked around the curtain, neither of us wanting to go out and start the evening. This was a disaster; it was actually costing us to be there, and we would be left with a large shortfall on the venue hire. All we could do was pray, *Okay, God, we're here. We feel this is a failure. We need You to show up.*

That night God did show up, and among that small crowd were some of the most heartfelt responses to the message of the gospel. At the end of the night, Nat and I repented and said, "Lord, help us to see how You see." What we called a failure was someone's night of salvation. In moments when we fail, we need to remember to widen the angle of our lens. Yes, we had failed to fill the room, and we had failed economically and logistically, but through God we had not failed spiritually.

Elijah had become so used to success in the Lord—calling down fire and outrunning chariots (see 1 Kings 18)—that when he faced the threat on his life from Jezebel, this prophet who had dared to do so much for God struggled in the face of failure.

> He came to a broom bush, sat down under it and prayed that he might die. "I have had enough, LORD," he said. "Take my life; I am no better than my ancestors" (1 Kings 19:4).

God instructed Elijah through an angel to get up and eat (verse 5). He needed to find a new perspective. He appeared to be throwing away everything that had happened up until that point because the failure he was facing was shrinking his outlook. Elijah had dared to step out, but now he needed to dare to fail well. He needed to find a new stamina and strength that wouldn't come from the adrenaline of performing miracles but rather from the awakening of something deeper within him.

Often when we feel like we are failing, we also lose our will to go on, and we allow exhaustion to overtake our decisions. Where before we would have pushed through, back when we were experiencing an adrenaline rush as things went well, now in the face of failure we back down. That's why we have to dare to fail, to keep the same intensity and commitment no matter how we feel.

For the first few years of Dare to Be, Nat and I would sit down after a tour and have the same conversation. We were exhausted, and I missed my kids, who were an ocean away. The constant travel, being in a different place every night, was wearing on both of us. We asked each other, "Are you ready to quit?"

We had decided at the start that we would never do something just for its own sake, and now we were tired and feeling in some ways that the tour hadn't been as successful as we had wanted. We took stock of the problems we had to handle, from venue issues to logistical nightmares to crazy storms that were completely out of our control but made some of the events virtually impossible to put on. In our weariness, we could recall the failures much more quickly than the successes.

That's the thing about failure; it likes to intimidate you and then persuade you that maybe now is the time to quit—just like what happened to Elijah. Failure starts to counsel you in a way that is often final.

After talking late into the night, Nat and I would say, "Let's just sleep on it and see how we feel tomorrow." It's amazing how that space between exhaustion and decisions can be so critical. In that time, we realized that the answer wasn't to quit; the answer was to learn to be okay with failing at times. In the loss is a gain; in the setback is the opportunity for a comeback.

Let me remind you of Peter. He felt that he had failed; perhaps he thought he no longer qualified to be a disciple. After his denial of Jesus, we see him going back to his fishing boat, back to the place where he first found his calling and his identity. When Jesus initially called Peter, it was after an unsuccessful night's fishing (Luke 5:1-11), and now here is Peter once again, and we see a similar scene play out. There's the boat, no fish, and Jesus—whom Peter doesn't recognize at this point—helping him find the catch that had eluded him.

> "I'm going out to fish," Simon Peter told them, and they said, "We'll go with you." So they went out and got into the boat, but that night they caught nothing.
>
> Early in the morning, Jesus stood on the shore, but the disciples did not realize that it was Jesus.
>
> He called out to them, "Friends, haven't you any fish?"

In the loss is a gain;

in the setback is

the opportunity

for a comeback.

"No," they answered.

He said, "Throw your net on the right side of the boat and you will find some." When they did, they were unable to haul the net in because of the large number of fish (John 21:3-6).

Sometimes, when failure happens, we just need help to get back in the game, to get back to what we are called to do. Jesus met Peter in a familiar place to remind him of his call, not his fall. Jesus was about to teach him that in the moments following failure, you don't quit, don't exit the plan, don't revert to a former way of life—instead, you dare to try again. Dare to drop your nets once more, dare to reenter the beginning of your calling.

Jesus was about to ask Peter to go again, serve again, get involved again, trust again. Like Peter, when we have experienced failure, we need to put our net back in, sign back up, open our life again, get connected again.

Peter was the one who would try anything—he was the one who had tried to walk on water! (See Matthew 14:22-33.) When we revisit that story, how quick we are to focus on the fact that he started to sink. The truth is, he took a step; he may have failed to keep walking, but he didn't fail to try, and he experienced something the others who stayed in the boat never would.

Here again in John 21, when Peter saw it was Jesus on the shore, he had to make a choice to stay in the boat or get back into the water. That's a choice we all have when we fail. We can stay dry and safe, or we can risk looking like fools and jump in again. Peter knew this was Jesus, and it was time to reenter the water.

The disciple whom Jesus loved said to Peter, "It is the Lord!" As soon as Simon Peter heard him say, "It is the Lord," he wrapped his outer garment around him (for he had taken it off) and jumped into the water (verse 7).

You, too, must dare to get back in the water. Don't go steadily. Jump in. Your enthusiasm is contagious—when you dive in, others will follow. Don't let the enemy tell you to calm down. Don't let failure stop you; instead, understand that it is part of what is shaping you.

When we understand that failing is part of following, we can see the moments when we want to exit as opportunities to reenter our commitment. God is gracious. He is not finished with us; the best is yet to come. Whatever God has asked us to do, we need to keep that commitment. God doesn't wave a finger; He creates a fire. He re-ignites that passion within us.

Jesus went as far as setting up a fire for Peter and the other disciples present, cooking them breakfast and then asking Peter the same question three times.

> When they had finished eating, Jesus said to Simon Peter, "Simon son of John, do you love me more than these?"
>
> "Yes, Lord," he said, "you know that I love you."
>
> Jesus said, "Feed my lambs."
>
> Again Jesus said, "Simon son of John, do you love me?"
>
> He answered, "Yes, Lord, you know that I love you."
>
> Jesus said, "Take care of my sheep."
>
> The third time he said to him, "Simon son of John, do you love me?"
>
> Peter was hurt because Jesus asked him the third time, "Do you love me?" He said, "Lord, you know all things; you know that I love you."
>
> Jesus said, "Feed my sheep" (John 21:15-17).

Get back

in the water.

Don't go steadily.

Jump in.

Every time Peter answered "yes," Jesus reminded him of his calling. Jesus did this three times—after Peter had denied Him three times. Perhaps Jesus wanted him to use the failing to establish something that would help hold him in the times when he was sure to face failure again. When you feel people have failed you or you have failed people, you must dare to talk through and process those moments.

Recently my husband and I had another building project on our property; we decided to build a little writer's room at the end of our garden. The plan was discussed and the concrete was poured, and then I had to go work on some projects with Nat for Dare to Be in the United States. I left my husband and the builders to get on with the job.

Ten days later I returned home and looked across the garden at the room that was now well along in the building process. I asked my husband, "Maybe it's my jet lag or just my eyesight, but babe, is that house sideways?"

Yep, the whole writer's room had somehow been built at an angle. I don't know where the plan began to fail, but as the failure had been ignored and more wood had been added, everything ended up at a slant. My husband said, "Well, I thought it looked a little off, but I just assumed they knew what they were doing."

Right there is where the problem often lies. When we don't want to face failure, we end up building something that just isn't quite right. Maybe it's in a relationship where we choose not to face that offense. Maybe it's in a ministry where we avoid the issue that is now affecting the integrity of the work.

The failure of our writer's room was evident, but it had been ignored. Now we had a choice to make: live with it or admit that it was wrong and start over. The next day that room had to be deconstructed so we could begin again.

When we refuse to face the failure, we leave ourselves vulnerable, and we give the enemy a foothold so that in the future he can exploit what we chose not to address.

Let's not be afraid to fail. Let's not hold back because the risk of failing is too great. Failure happens. Every great inventor, every world changer, will tell you they failed more than they succeeded. The problem is that we often play up the win and downplay the loss—but without daring to fail, there is no victory to share. If we allowed the fear of failure to govern all our decisions, we wouldn't even leave our living rooms and get on the tour bus. Failure is not the end; it's the place where we have to dare to go again.

NOTES FROM NATALIE

It would be fair to say that Dare to Be has introduced both Charl and me to the necessity of daring to fail. Whenever things have gone more wrong than right, we have learned to lean in, commit to grow stronger, and step out again.

Of course, it's so easy to focus on the tragedy. In every season, we talk and talk about what has gone wrong. In our human nature, it's almost impossible to look at tragedy as being a good thing. But it's helpful to stop for a second and refocus. Instead of seeing everything bad as from the enemy and everything good as from God, let's try to look at failure as the place of our victory.

Jonah experienced the ultimate failure, being thrown overboard and swallowed by a big fish. But that time in the belly of the fish was where God brought triumph from his tragedy.

> From inside the fish Jonah prayed to the LORD his God. He said:
>
>> "In my distress I called to the LORD,
>>   and he answered me.
>> From deep in the realm of the dead I called for help,
>>   and you listened to my cry" (Jonah 2:1-2).

It was in the midst of his failure that Jonah called out to God, and God heard his cry. Jonah would never have experienced the repentance of the city of Nineveh without his time in the depths of the ocean. This failure wasn't defining; it was refining—and it can be the same for us today.

When I received the diagnosis of thyroid cancer, I faced the very real possibility that my voice would be taken from me. My song "Who Else" captures my journey to hold on to the truth that God can take a tragedy and turn it into my gateway for victory. That cancer diagnosis was exactly what God used to propel me to the place He wanted me to be.

While we are looking for a way out of the fire, God is looking at what He can bring from the fire. While we are looking for a way out of the storm, God is looking at what He can bring from the storm. Who else can take a tragedy and turn it into victory? Only God can do this.

None of us run out to embrace failure. But when it happens in your life, instead of letting that failure define you, consider how it will refine you. God is going to take that failure, because He never fails, and He will turn it around for your good. So you don't have to be devastated; instead, you can allow God to do His work of victory.

Let's own this truth today. Take your eyes off your failure and bravely allow God to help you adjust the lens, letting you see how your disappointment can become a place where you encounter the One who never fails. Dare to worship even in the worst of times, knowing there is no one like our God—and He can and will work all things together for our good (Romans 8:28).

You are not afraid of the fire
'Cause You can bring these ashes back to life
When I am surrounded by flames
I have this confidence when nothing else makes sense

Who else can take a tragedy
And turn it into victory?
Who else? Who else?
Who is like You, God
Who takes the worst that life can bring
And use it all for Your glory?
Who else? Who else?
Who is like You, God?

You are never shaken by the wind
'Cause You can build the broken up again
When I have lost all my strength to stand
I have this confidence when nothing else makes sense

You never fail; You never will
You're working everything together for my good
You never fail; You never will
You're bringing turnaround just like You said You would[7]

QUESTIONS FOR DISCUSSION AND REFLECTION

- When have you been afraid to fail?

- In the future, what can you do to replace fear with faith?

- Where do you need to jump back into your dream?

8

DARE TO SHARE

Natalie and I became used to navigating the curveballs thrown in our direction. We had made a commitment to keep going because we were more convinced than ever before that what we had dared to begin and build was now becoming a vessel for blessing many lives. On the other side of our failures, we discovered a new level of flourishing.

We knew a message like "Dare to be" would attract people at different stages of their journeys some just stepping out and daring to believe God for more, and others who were well on the way of daring to build the dream they had held for years. Nat and I were constantly aware of those in the room who had dared to keep going and didn't quit despite having to face some of the worst situations and challenges imaginable.

These women were still worshipping, still serving, still making a difference even though their own stories were filled with heartache and brokenness. They had discovered something others needed them to dare to share. They had been through the most testing of circumstances, and yet somehow found the strength to keep moving. They could preach and testify louder because they were the living proof that God is faithful even when life is so unfair.

We can allow the perceived successes of those around us to tell us that our journey doesn't measure up, that the challenges we have faced should be hidden and remain unspoken. The enemy wants to attach shame to our struggles and make us feel embarrassed of the rough parts of our life. He doesn't want us to dare to share those seasons with others, because he knows that when we start to share, we overcome. As Revelation 12:11 (KJV) puts it, "They overcame him by the blood of the Lamb, and by the word of their testimony."

There are two parts to our overcoming; God took care of His part, and we are responsible for ours. Your testimony is part of your victory. Your willingness to share allows you to extract the seed from your sorrow and plant it for tomorrow. What you have been through can help another find breakthrough. The enemy hates when you share your life, your lessons, your story because he knows they will bring your Redeemer, your Healer, your Savior all the glory.

If Nat and I really wanted to dare women to be all God had called them to be, then we needed those women who had overcome to share so others could also dare. So a plan began to form as we sat on the tour bus one day. We wanted to find a way for women to share their triumph in the midst of the most trying times, to share how they had found strength in the storms of life. We began to imagine creating a space at every event where we could honor someone's story by sharing about a woman's faith and tenacity. We could take the spotlight off the stage where we were standing and put it over the life of someone who, despite everything, had stood strong. We had no idea how we would make this happen, but we were determined to find a way.

That's how the Dare to Be Foundation was born. We decided to find a woman at each event location and tell her story. We knew this type of heroine wouldn't want a fuss to be made over her. She wouldn't seek the applause or

Your testimony

is part of

your victory.

the approval of others. So for this to work, we were going to need to get those around her to share her story. To make it even more fun, we wanted them to do it secretly, so we could then surprise the woman with a moment we prayed would add strength to her weary, beautiful soul. We needed helpers, lots of them—women who would take the time to nominate another woman in their world to be honored and celebrated at our Dare to Be event.

In our modern world, we have replaced honor with criticism and competition. We have become cynical, and we therefore withhold honor from one another. But the beauty and power of this biblical principle holds true. In Romans 12:10, the apostle Paul tells us, "Be devoted to one another in love. Honor one another above yourselves."

We wanted these moments in our events to bring honor back. To create a space where all the words spoken brought honor to an incredible woman, where an entire room of strangers would recognize the story of a sister in Christ.

We had a plan, and now we needed to put that plan into action. We started asking for nominations; we were daring women to share with us the story of someone they knew and loved. We used radio spots to advertise the idea to the local communities where we were headed next. And not long after that, our first nominations came rolling in.

It was humbling to sit on the bus and read about the nominations, to hear how people had faced so much adversity. There were stories of a single parent raising her children while also battling her own illness and taking care of others in her community, and a recently bereaved parent who lost her child and was now helping others in their grief. There were stories of ones who had fought for freedom from addiction and abuse. These stories provided testimony after testimony of what it looked like to dare to be in the face of adversity. They were weapons of faith that could help those who were shackled by fear. They were anchors of hope that could steady the life of someone who felt tossed by the waves of hopelessness. These stories had power that could become someone else's permission to carry on.

Nat and I now had nominations, but we needed God's guidance to decide which women we should honor and what we should do to honor them. Like all things we dare to begin, we just had to take one step at a time. We knew we wanted to do something to bless those women, but how could we do that well?

If you believe in something, you also have to be willing to invest in it. I remember Nat and I getting out our checkbooks and saying, "Okay, what can we do to show some kindness to these women?" We couldn't do everything, but we certainly could do something.

While we were excited, we were also apprehensive about adding this honor moment into our event. What if the honoree didn't show up, since she wouldn't know she was going to be honored? Or what if when we called her name, she didn't want to come forward? What if the women in the room didn't get behind this?

The what-if can be our worst enemy. Often the reason we don't share our journey, our time, our finances, our kindness is because we wonder, *What if when I share, the response is not what I want it to be?*

But sharing, of course, isn't about what we want it to be. As a child, your parents probably told you it was good to share. You may have had other ideas. Maybe you were pretty sure that the person you had to share with wouldn't treat your toys with the same care you did. And sure enough, when you shared, that friend was careless; they bumped the scooter or tore a page in the book. Sharing is daring because what you share, you allow others to shape.

Anyone who knows me knows that when I offer to share my muffin, I have an idea in my mind of how that split will look. I'm happy to share the bottom, but the top of the muffin is mine. I am sharing, but with an unspoken ideal in my head of what that sharing should look like. Perhaps you have stopped sharing your life, time, energy, and money because when you did so in the past, the out-come wasn't what you anticipated. So now you have decided it's easier just to withhold those things. That's what the enemy wants: to neutralize the power of your testimony, to stop anyone else benefiting from your life and journey.

It's time to turn the what-if around and change the question. Flip the conversation from "What if it doesn't work?" to "What if it *does*?" Nat and I chose to wonder, *What if the woman is in the room and this is exactly what she needs? What if she not only comes forward but helps others step forward? What if the other women in the room get so behind this honoring moment that they pray and stand with her for a miracle?*

That first night we honored a beautiful woman and shared her story of overcoming loss and tragedy. Everyone in the room was weeping as we shared, and as she came to the platform to be honored, the whole group spontaneously jumped to their feet and applauded as this sister walked down the aisle. It was such a powerful moment. Nat and I then gave her some gifts: money for spa treatments, a gift card for her to go treat herself, a hamper of goodies, and flowers. She was overwhelmed with those simple gestures. The Dare to Be Foundation had been launched, and yet we sensed we hadn't seen anything yet.

A few weeks later we discussed these moments, feeling a little frustrated that we couldn't do more for every deserving woman. That's when I felt God remind me of the story of the boy who dared to share his loaves and fish (John 6:1-13). Jesus needed to feed a massive crowd, and I am sure most people felt that they couldn't help. I mean, what's the point of sharing what seems so little when the problem is so big? But one young boy donated his loaves and fish, perhaps thinking, *I can't take care of everyone, but I can help someone.*

So I said to Nat, "Why don't we ask the women in the room if they want to help us make this happen? Why don't we ask them if they will share in this moment too? And what if they would be willing to give and pay it forward to honor a woman in the next place we are headed? They would be giving to someone they had never met, and they wouldn't even know the story in advance. But they would be saying, 'If my loaves and fish can become a miracle for someone else, I'm in.'"

We decided at the very last minute to add a moment to the next event when we would ask if the women in attendance wanted to help us. Now, when I say this was a last-minute decision, I mean we hadn't even thought about how we would collect any of those donations from the women. So we ended up having someone from the team run out and find a roll of garbage bags. Yes, you read that right—garbage bags were used to collect the offering. And we didn't have anyone designated to do the collection; our team consisted of band members and light and audio techs, so we had to get a few people from behind the scenes to help pass the bags along the aisles.

I remember standing on the stage and sharing our heart about what we wanted to do, and I soon became distracted by women grabbing their handbags and pulling out their wallets. They were ready to join the dare. They wanted to be a part of this moment with us. That night we filled the garbage bags as people generously gave. Thinking back, it must have been the funniest scene with Nat and me, a couple members of our team, and my teenage daughter who had accompanied us all walking back to the bus carrying garbage bags of cash. We honestly looked like we had just robbed a bank. We then sat on the floor of the bus, counting the donated money so we could deposit it in the bank the next morning. That night, it seemed God had let us know loud and clear that this wasn't just a good idea—it was a God idea. He was going to multiply the loaves and fish the women had shared in a way that would change people's lives in the most beautiful ways.

From that point forward, the Dare to Be Foundation has given (at the time of writing) over half a million dollars' worth of gifts to deserving women. This includes Braille equipment for a lovely young woman who tragically lost her sight and was about to start university. It includes building a playground in honor of two children who had been killed by a drunk driver while they had been playing on the sidewalk, as there had been no communal area where they could play. It includes paying the medical bills for a woman who had not only fought her own illness but had taken care of her family and other sick friends in the midst of her struggles.

What started with a moment when a room full of women dared to share has become a movement of kindness as each city we visit pays it forward to the next.

STUCK IN LO DEBAR

Life can be so unfair at times. And those unfair circumstances can keep us from sharing our life, from giving to bless someone else's life because we wonder, *What about me?* It takes a bold decision to say, "Despite what I am going through, I am going to choose to let God bless others through whatever I have." That's brave, and that's actually the key to our breakthrough.

In the book of 2 Samuel we read about a man named Mephibosheth, whose life took a very unfortunate twist. He found himself relocated to a place called Lo Debar. The name Lo Debar means a place of no pasture, a place of no words, a place of no thing. Perhaps as you read this you are feeling that you and Mephibosheth are in the same neighborhood.

This young man's life should have looked so different. He was the son of Jonathan, the grandson of King Saul. When he was only five, news arrived that both his father and grandfather had died on the battlefield. This boy was left fatherless and his home was going to come under attack. Now he had to run for his life.

He was five years old when the news about Saul and Jonathan came from Jezreel. His nurse picked him up and fled, but as she hurried to leave, he fell and became disabled (2 Samuel 4:4).

The nurse who was supposed to be looking after Mephibosheth dropped him in her hurry to escape. This young boy went from prince to fugitive, from able bodied to disabled, from living as royalty to ending up in Lo Debar. His whole world changed overnight.

Perhaps you can relate to that scenario; out of the blue came the news you didn't expect, the revelation you didn't imagine, the betrayal you didn't perceive. These life twists start to close us down, and we begin to believe we no longer have anything to give. We allow the things that happened to us to steal the hope that is within us. The more those circumstances affect our lives, the less of our lives we want to share.

Mephibosheth lost his title, but he did not lose his value. The enemy wants to shut you down; he wants you to believe the lie that your significance is attached to your status. But the label life gives you does not alter the value within you. You might be a former addict, but that is not what God calls you. You might have gone from happily married to single parent, employed to unemployed, wealthy to broke. Those things may have happened in your life, but they don't define you.

If status had been the significance of people in the Bible, the stories would read very differently. Look at Mary—her status was an unwed young mother, yet her destiny was to be the chosen carrier of our Savior. How wrongly labeled she must have been by those around her when God had called and chosen her. Even Jesus was given a label: "Isn't this the carpenter's son?" (Matthew 13:55). In that place where they limited Him, they wouldn't allow Him to share the good things He wanted to bring.

The label life

gives you does

not alter the

value within you.

You cannot allow your status to undervalue your significance. You still have worth; there are things you still need to dare to be, dare to give, dare to share.

In the story of Mephibosheth, we find that God placed this young man on King David's mind.

> The king asked, "Is there no one still alive from the house of Saul to whom I can show God's kindness?"
>
> Ziba answered the king, "There is still a son of Jonathan; he is lame in both feet."
>
> "Where is he?" the king asked.
>
> Ziba answered, "He is at the house of Makir son of Ammiel in Lo Debar" (2 Samuel 9:3-4).

When we live with a willingness to release, we become part of God's plan of increase. King David was about to share with a man he didn't even know, a man living in the place called Lo Debar, a man who was stuck in very unfair circumstances. David was about to help relocate Mephibosheth through an act of kindness—and this is what we have seen happen in every honoree moment at Dare to Be events. It's the willingness of a friend to tell the story of someone living in a Lo Debar situation. It's the willingness of women to give so help can be sent. It's the willingness of each honored woman to share her life so others can find hope for the future.

When we create these moments in the room at Dare to Be, there is always an overwhelming reaction from the ones being honored. Some women fall on their knees, cry out loud, start shouting out. Others simply stand, lost for words and shaking from head to toe. Kindness is powerful, and it has the ability to bring healing. It's a reminder that God sees us in every season—and though Lo Debar may be one woman's current location, it is not her final destination.

We can't let the things that have happened to us become the prison that keeps us.

> The LORD is my shepherd, I lack nothing.
> He makes me lie down in green pastures,
>   he leads me beside quiet waters,
>   he refreshes my soul.
> He guides me along the right paths
>   for his name's sake.
> Even though I walk
>   through the darkest valley,
> I will fear no evil (Psalm 23:1-4).

If you are in Lo Debar and there's no pasture, no place to lie down, you have to keep moving. If that movement just looks like taking one step, take it. Don't make a passing place your permanent address. Don't lose your voice in the valley. Don't allow the storm to steal your strength. Dare to keep moving, keep praying, keep worshipping, keep committing, keep sharing.

My favorite part of Mephibosheth's story is what comes next. Once the king has him at the palace, David lets Mephibosheth know of the kindness he wants to extend to him. Besides all the land that will be restored to Mephibosheth, David dares to share one more thing: He invites him to dine evermore at the king's table (2 Samuel 9:7).

That was not an honor extended to everybody; this gift was very personal. Dining at the king's table would give Mephibosheth a greater place of standing and influence than possessions ever could. Suddenly this man whom everyone saw as the lame one was now seated at the king's table and would have to be addressed with honor and dignity.

When we share a woman's story at Dare to Be and then say her name out

When we live

with a willingness

to release, we

become part of God's

plan of increase.

loud, the whole group gets up and starts applauding as she makes her way to the stage. When she speaks to the thousands gathered, the atmosphere shifts. Her words have an authority. What the enemy wanted to use to destroy her is being used as a weapon to destroy him.

We overcome by the power of our testimony. That's why we need to share—because when we do, we place what we have into the hands of the King, and He uses our little to feed a lot more lives. He uses our song, our story, our gift, and our willingness to start a ripple of kindness.

NOTES FROM NATALIE

One of my favorite things about the honor moment at a Dare to Be event is seeing how the honoree has become vulnerable with her own story. She has realized that she doesn't have to hide her circumstances; she has been generous with her pain. It has cost her to share like this, but she has chosen to invite people into her life. By doing this, she has built them up.

Our sovereign God shares His suffering with us to encourage us in our struggles. Back when I wrote the song "No Stranger," I meditated on a passage of Scripture from Psalm 8.

> O LORD, our Lord, your majestic name fills the earth!
>   Your glory is higher than the heavens.
> You have taught children and infants
>   to tell of your strength,
> silencing your enemies
>   and all who oppose you.
> When I look at the night sky and see the work of your fingers—
>   the moon and the stars you set in place—

> what are mere mortals that you should think about them,
> 　human beings that you should care for them?
> Yet you made them only a little lower than God
> 　and crowned them with glory and honor (Psalm 8:1-5 NLT).

Yet. Don't you love that word? The King of all is the One who has always been and always will be, from the beginning to the end, the full authority of all things. *Yet* He made us, and when He made us, He crowned us "with glory and honor." Yes, we experience heartbreak; yes, we can go through seasons of drought when we pray and pray for rain to fall. *Yet* God made us.

And just like us, Jesus was wounded, and He doesn't hide His scars from us. When we are afraid, when we are hurting, what an incredible reality to know that our God is no stranger to hardship. He, too, understands a raging storm.

You have a seat at the King's table. You are called by name. Just as we recognize the journey of each incredible woman we honor at Dare to Be, God sees you, and He values every part of your story. You are no stranger to Him. Let that truth give you a newfound authority and a certainty of your identity in Christ.

Will you dare to share, to make yourself vulnerable in order to help others through their hardships? Listen for the voice that whispers, "Peace, be still" (Mark 4:39 KJV), then use your pain to bring breakthrough for someone in your world today. Let the words of this song become strength for your soul. God is no stranger to whatever situation you are facing.

You are no stranger to the scar
So You can have my wounded heart
You weren't protected from the pain
So You can hold me when I break

You seek me out and find me here
With love that knows the taste of tears
So I will trust in who You are
You're no stranger
No stranger to the scar

You are no stranger to the storm
You have calmed these winds before
Your voice still whispers, "Peace, be still"
And the waves still do Your will

So I won't fear the rising tide
The tempest roars and You arrive
I'll walk on these angry seas
For You're no stranger
You're no stranger, Lord, to me[8]

QUESTIONS FOR DISCUSSION AND REFLECTION

- How can you change your what-if from a negative to a positive?

- What do you need to release so you can increase?

- What would it look like for you to leave Lo Debar?

9

DARE TO TRUST

The adventure of daring will only be as great as the depth of your trusting. This whole Dare to Be journey, from the first day God put the lives of two strangers together to the ongoing ministry we are building today, has been and still is a continual trust test. We are daring to trust God, to trust the plan we sense He is writing, to trust the Holy Spirit's nudge that at times makes no sense to our minds and yet finds an *amen* in our hearts.

Natalie and I have had to dare to trust: to trust each other, to trust the process that often seems more inconvenient than convenient, and to trust God for provision, our families' well-being, our health, our future. By accepting God's invitation to take this journey, we have had to be willing to let our plans be adjusted. For some, that may be an easy thing to accept, but when you are a planner like me, that's a bigger challenge.

My life once ran on my lists—the allowances I made within my schedule so that my time and energy would be well spent. I would even leave lists on our fridge every time I went away so everyone could stay on track with who needed to be where on what day. Yep, I know how to plan.

When God interrupts such plans, we soon find out where our trust lies. We either trust in our way or trust in God's way. Trusting God means we must do what we say we believe, which may mean tearing up some lists we have so carefully written.

Have you ever had to do a trust fall? It might have been part of a team-building exercise at work or something you did at school with your friends. Trust falls involve standing with your back to the people who have volunteered to catch you and then falling backward, completely dependent on them to break your fall. It doesn't seem hard when you are talking about doing it beforehand; you can see the faces of those who will catch you, and they let you know they won't drop you. But once you turn your back and can no longer see those reassuring expressions, it feels very different. Now you have to let yourself fall without actually being able to see if the others are where they said they would be.

That experience is exactly what this whole journey of Dare to Be has felt like—one big trust fall. Along the way Nat and I have both sensed God asking us to let go of some of the things we have become so accustomed to holding on to for safety. He's asked us to learn to trust His voice, to keep moving even though we can't see what comes next, to fall into His faithfulness and leave behind our often-hidden safety harnesses.

Safety harnesses come in many shapes and sizes—from the relationships we depend on to get us through, to the plan B we make in case God doesn't come through. Our harnesses are the lifeboats we are ready to jump into if the ship seems to be sinking. They are there to ensure that if this doesn't work out as we are hoping, we have a backup plan.

TWO OFFERINGS

Jesus commented on these two approaches to life as He watched people giving their offerings.

> As Jesus looked up, he saw the rich putting their gifts into the temple treasury. He also saw a poor widow put in two very small copper coins. "Truly I tell you," he said, "this poor widow has put in more than all the others. All these people gave their gifts out of their wealth; but she out of her poverty put in all she had to live on" (Luke 21:1-4).

Jesus saw the rich people come and give their large donations, and then He observed the widow give her two coins. He saw some give with safety harnesses firmly attached. These offerings were something they could afford. They were budgeted for, and these people had provision at home for other needs. Such giving was not coming from a place of trusting, but from a place of safety. The widow, however, gave all she had. She had no safety harness, no separate funds for a rainy day, nothing left. This gift was her free fall of trusting, and Jesus immediately recognized it.

How often in life does our giving, serving, or obedience look like that widow's? How often do we dare to trust God with what we have, dare to fall into His faithfulness and make this journey through life that much more adventurous? Are we more like the ones who gave but kept some in reserve, who were generous because they did not need to trust? How much are we doing in our own strength, and how much are we completely trusting to God's power and grace?

The trust test is when you are in that widow's shoes. It's a place where you think, *If I do this, I don't know what will happen next.* Too many of us say we trust God while, in reality, we're clinging to the things that will break our fall. We all experience times when our trust is abused, when someone we think will catch us doesn't, when the thing we placed such great faith in fails. The one who promised "forever" leaves. The pledge is broken. The promotion promised is denied. The leader lets us down. When we feel mistreated, we start to add our own safety harnesses; we say, "That will never happen to me again." And in order to make sure it doesn't, we start to trust less and question more.

Unfortunately, that same behavior can become a barrier rather than a protection when we transfer our lack of trust to God. We often allow many other untrustworthy voices to lead and guide our lives. We listen to advice from social media influencers, political idealists, lifestyle gurus, and a cacophony of other advisers—but all this noise becomes overwhelming and a diversion from the one true voice readily available for us to hear in the pages of Scripture.

When God invites us to dare to trust Him, we unknowingly begin to apply the same safety precautions we have developed to protect our plans. Instead of embracing the adventure He has for us, we want God Almighty, Yahweh, to sign our health and safety waiver first.

God is a good Father. He is patient and kind, and He knows you. The dare He is asking you to take is one He knows you can make. The step that feels like such a test of trust is one He knows you have the strength to take.

PUTTING OUT A FLEECE

Gideon asked God to sign his waiver.

God had asked Gideon to trust Him by going in the strength he had (Judges 6:14). But as Gideon was embarking on this new adventure, he had a moment when the dare to trust caused him to feel the need for a harness. He asked for something that seems so strange to us and yet also so familiar.

Gideon wanted to trust God in the battle he knew he was called to begin, and yet he wanted God to send him a sign. He put out a fleece so God could show him that He was going to catch him if he took this trust fall.

> Gideon said to God, "If you will save Israel by my hand as you have promised—look, I will place a wool fleece on the threshing floor. If there is dew only on the fleece and all the ground is dry, then I will know that you will save Israel by my hand, as you said." And that is what happened. Gideon rose early the next day; he squeezed the fleece and wrung out the dew—a bowlful of water (Judges 6:36-38).

You would think this response would be enough, but Gideon asked God for a second sign—realizing he might be pushing it a little far.

> Gideon said to God, "Do not be angry with me. Let me make just one more request. Allow me one more test with the fleece, but this time make the fleece dry and let the ground be covered with dew." That night God did so. Only the fleece was dry; all the ground was covered with dew (verses 39-40).

God was gracious to Gideon and responded, and in the morning Gideon marched into battle.

We can all create those fleece moments: "God, if this person calls me it will be a sign"; "God, if I get this opportunity I will know it's a sign." We forget that Gideon did not need a fleece. He had already been given the word; God had already shown up in his world. Gideon had the strength to take the step, and he just needed the faith to take the trust fall. You can add so many extras to your life that will stop you from ever daring to trust, so maybe it's time to put away your fortieth fleece and trust the One who is on the other side of this trust fall.

I think if you had asked Nat and me separately before this Dare to Be adventure if we trusted God, we would have said, "Yes, totally." But launching this ministry was the litmus test. We had to dare not to trust our own planning and scheduling and management systems, but instead to trust the God who knows us better than we know ourselves. The God who, before we ever made one plan, had seen all the plans He had for us.

We are told in Scripture,

> Trust in the LORD with all your heart
> and lean not on your own understanding (Proverbs 3:5).

Trusting with all your heart is a continual journey. So often we speak of trust in one sentence and express dependence on our own abilities in the next. That's why daring to trust is something we have to commit to over and over again. When we can't comprehend God's ways, we default to ours; when we fail to see Him as our source, we place trust in our own resources. But our trust is linked to our revelation of whom we are trusting. The more we come to know the One who will catch us, the more we will find the courage to take the leap He invites us to take.

LEAVING NO DELAY

One of the ultimate trust tests we see unfold in Scripture is the test that Joshua faced—a test that would challenge not only his obedience but also his loyalty and his own ideas of wisdom. As he faced the great city of Jericho, Joshua had to dare to trust God for his people's safety and future. The steps he was asked to take left a lot more questions than answers—and that's often where

Our trust is

linked to our

revelation of whom

we are trusting.

we all face our first sticking point. It's the overthinking that gets in the way of daring.

Joshua was following in the very big footsteps of Moses, and soon after he led the people of Israel into the promised land, he faced his greatest challenge yet: the walled city of Jericho. The Lord gave him a battle plan that sounded crazy.

> March around the city once with all the armed men. Do this for six days. Have seven priests carry trumpets of rams' horns in front of the ark. On the seventh day, march around the city seven times, with the priests blowing the trumpets. When you hear them sound a long blast on the trumpets, have the whole army give a loud shout; then the wall of the city will collapse and the army will go up, everyone straight in (Joshua 6:3-5).

I don't know how you would respond, but I know I would be asking a lot of questions. I would stall with a long conversation and some negotiations for a backup plan. That's why Joshua is an example when it comes to daring to trust; his first and only response wasn't to ask for more information but to immediately get ready to act. In the very next verses, Joshua gathers the priests and soldiers to share the plan, ordering, "Advance!" (verse 7).

Between God's instruction and his obedience, apparently Joshua left no delay. But I have often let a delay deny me of an opportunity that trust extended to me. I have often widened the gap between instruction and obedience to such an extent that the instruction becomes just an optional inconvenience to me. But in this passage, Joshua made sure the gap was small. He heard from God and then prepared for battle. He did not allow days and weeks to go by while he discussed with others what he thought he heard God say. He surely realized that to widen the conversation was to invite contamination, which could then lead to intimidation rather than obedience.

God knew the plans He had for Joshua—that he would lead God's chosen people, that his example would speak to generations, and that his trusting would become fuel for others who followed. Joshua was confident that God's ways were great and His love and faithfulness were deep. Joshua trusted God as Father, and he led Israel in an act of obedience.

Circling the walls of Jericho without a word for seven days was a trust test. Each time the people went around, Joshua likely had to navigate the urge to prepare more, explain more, do *something*. But he had a deep certainty that God would provide for Israel in the battle, no matter how long the odds. And his trust test at Jericho was a reminder to us that battles aren't just won by conventional wisdom, but by the power of the Almighty.

When we can believe God not just for our own lives but for our loved ones, we trust more. When our trust in Him goes deeper, the dare we are willing to take goes further. The dare to trust is also the invitation to discover more of God.

DARING TO CONTINUE

Nat and I were on that journey of trusting God in new areas. We were learning to trust His voice when things made no sense on paper, trusting His plans were higher. When others advised us to act differently, we dared to continue with what we felt God had spoken to us privately. In the whole process we had scary moments and also deeply secure moments. We were seeing on a regular basis that when we took the trust fall, God would catch us in the most beautiful ways.

We got to a point where we needed to have another bus for our crew. The Dare to Be event was growing, and that meant we needed a bigger team to pull it off—and everyone was feeling a little cramped on the bus. We had no budget for an extra vehicle; we just sensed this was something we needed to make happen as we stepped out in faith. We needed all those people on the road with us, and we needed to make sure we took care of them. So we booked an extra tour bus, adding thousands of dollars to our total costs. As we made the commitment, we prayed, *God, You said to go for this, and we need You to help us go. We need provision for this vision.*

A few weeks later, we got the news that we had received a check from a donor who wanted to bless our team and help us take care of expenses. They had asked if they could cover some of the transportation costs, and they wrote a check that covered the entire price of that bus for our next tour run. We had been so scared to take this step, but God had already made a plan to provide for us. Until we took the dare, though, the resources did not appear.

Why doesn't God share His plans sooner? Because *sooner* doesn't allow you to take your trust deeper. God wants you to swim in oceans of trust and not stay in the shallows of uncertainty. If you know everything up front, how is that daring? If you can see the next shore before you set off, how is that an adventure? God is not asking you to play it safe. He is asking you to change the world, to make a difference, to step out of your comfort zone and do something that brings people more of His life and love. To do this you have to be willing to trust Him in the deeper waters.

DEEPER WATERS

When I taught my children how to swim, they gradually moved from the shallows to the deep end. They went from their feet being able to touch the bottom of the pool to feeling that the floor was no longer there. Of course, it was there—I could feel it under my toes. But because of their shorter height, they

God wants you

to swim in oceans

of trust and not

stay in the shallows

of uncertainty.

had lost touch. Our experiences in the water were very different. I wasn't freaking out because I knew where the bottom of the pool was—but from their perspective, they were on their own.

That's how it is with God. Just because you can't feel the floor of the pool doesn't mean it's not there, but if you want to learn to swim, you have to go deeper. Your heavenly Father wants to lead you farther into the water, which means your feet must leave the security of the familiar.

Babies are incredible in the water. I remember taking one of my children, just months old, to a swim class, and the tutor encouraged everyone to let their babies go under the water. I thought that was the worst suggestion until I saw all the other moms place their babies in the water. There was no fear, just smiles and lots of squeals. The babies were not freaking out; they were doing what they were made to do. They were "swimming" before they had even started walking; they were fearless.

As I held my child in the water, I was reminded of how fearful I had been of swimming as a teenager. I remembered when I had to take swimming lessons at school; I was scared of going in the deep end and would do anything I could to avoid the part of the lesson when we had to put our heads under the water. How could my baby be in the water without panic, and yet as a teenager the same activity had filled me with fear?

We accumulate fear over time, and fear erodes our trust. Babies haven't entertained fear yet; they haven't started to converse with fear about the future and what is or isn't possible. Yet after only a few years, fear has offered a lot of unsolicited advice and depleted a lot of trust. So if we want to dare to trust then we have to be willing to deal with fear.

Joshua had faith in God, not fear. Joshua's faith was the enabler of his trust, and the same is true in all our lives. Over the past 15 years as friends, Nat and I have taken many trust tests together. We have learned to trust that God's plan is the right plan, that He is our provider when we feel the call to advance but the budget suggests we take a rest.

We have also learned to trust God's voice within each other. Over the years, this has been one of the most beautiful things to discover. I remember when we first faced some opposition to our plans and everything felt like it was harder than it should be. Nat and I were in two different parts of the world, and we both felt God speak to us separately about what to do next.

I was on a family vacation, and I had been doing a lot of private questioning over the future. Then I sensed God say, *Push ahead into this next part of the plan I have for you.*

About ten minutes later, my phone rang. It was Nat, and she said, "Listen, I was praying about everything, and I just felt like I should call you and say, 'God's got you, He's got this, and we should just push ahead.'"

Countless conversations like this one deepened our trust in God. When you trust God alongside someone else and come into agreement, something powerful happens. You don't blame each other if things get a little scary; you come together to fight for what you believe. You trust not just the other's gifts and skills but the God who is writing the bigger plan.

This trust led Nat and I to work in new, creative ways. For example, I would be in England creating a video piece for our Dare to Be opener, and Nat would be in the United States working on the flow of the worship and musical elements. We would be in different countries and time zones, trusting that God would guide us. It wouldn't be until months later that we would put these two things together and, every time, we would find we had the exact same message, the same emphasis being communicated. We were not just learning to trust God but also to deepen our trust as friends who have the same God within us.

Our trust needs daring; it's the only way it can start growing. We can all get stuck; our trust can become hijacked in an area of our life; we can experience trust issues in our relationships, our finances, our future. But if we want to write a different chapter, then we have to be open to a trust fall. Nat and I decided that we would rather fall into God's arms than fall into our plans. How about you?

NOTES FROM NATALIE

There have been, and there continue to be, so many elements of the Dare to Be journey that are beyond our control. Daring to trust has meant that from the moment God brought our lives together, Charl and I have had to exchange a sense of control for a deeper faith in our heavenly Father.

At such times, I have come before God in worship with the lyrics to "King of the World." Instead of trying to fit Him into a box that works for me, to say something was His will because it worked out according to my narrative, I have had to acknowledge that He is sovereign. Instead of trying to pull Him down so I can look Him in the eye, I have had to remind myself that my life is in the hands of the King of the world.

This doesn't come naturally to us because we tend to have an entirely different focus. We can be guilty of considering God our "BFF," focusing on the good things He provides for us and how He can hold us and protect us from harm. In our hearts we can move Him off His throne and onto a love seat with us.

We often talk about how God is our friend and encourager, but let's not lose sight of the fact that He is also sovereign. It's not either-or; it's both. God is concerned with everything about us and makes Himself known to us. But may we never forget that He is on His throne; He is our King who will reign forevermore. We can trust Him because, while our perspective is finite, He is infinite.

"My thoughts are not your thoughts,
   neither are your ways my ways,"
   declares the LORD.
"As the heavens are higher than the earth,
   so are my ways higher than your ways
   and my thoughts than your thoughts" (Isaiah 55:8-9).

It's our human nature, even when our conversations are centered around God, to make everything about us. But when everything is about Him, our perspective shifts from what He can do for us to who He is. That's when we take our trust fall, when we accept that He is working, even when we don't see it. That's when it gets to be all about Jesus.

Today, how can you dare to trust again? Where do you need to take that step or even a leap? Take some time to meditate on the infinite nature of our God. You will find your perspective begin to shift as you dare to trust the King of the world.

I try to fit You in the walls inside my mind
I try to keep You safely in between the lines
I try to put You in the box that I've designed
I try to pull You down so we are eye to eye

Just a whisper of Your voice can tame the seas
So who am I to try to take the lead?
Still, I run ahead and think I'm strong enough
When You're the One who made me from the dust

When did I forget You've always
been the King of the world?
I try to take life back, right out of the hands
of the King of the world
How could I make You so small
When You're the One who holds it all?
When did I forget You've always
been the King of the world?[9]

QUESTIONS FOR DISCUSSION AND REFLECTION

- In what areas of your life do you need to deepen your trust in God?

- Whose voice has the loudest volume in your life?

- In what ways do you need to move from the shallows to deeper waters?

10

DARE TO DARE AGAIN

So what's next? After you have dared to believe and begun to build, after you have chosen to share and stepped out in trust, where does the daring end? When do you take back the pen and write the words *The End*?

The answer to that question, friend, rests within you. The dare you take can be either an occasional excursion or your personal trainer. I have had a gym membership a few times in my life—perhaps you have too. I usually sign up for this commitment in January, when the Christmas calories have done their best work on my thighs and it's time to reintroduce my legs to some exercise.

Typically, I would enter the gym at the start of a new year with boldness, daring to put on the Lycra and embarrass myself by using all the machines incorrectly. At those times I was willing to risk losing a little dignity for the promise of feeling healthier. If I wasn't motivated enough by the thought of growing stronger, I had backup inspiration: the knowledge that I had invested money in this decision and needed to make sure my investment wouldn't be wasted.

However, after a while I found the same pattern occurring: My attendance at the gym dropped, and neither the desire to get fit nor the need for good stewardship seemed to be that important anymore…and my thighs, well, they were something I would rather accommodate than address.

My experience with the gym has a lot of parallels with our faith journey. If *daring to be* were your new membership to help you get spiritually fit, to stretch and build some new muscle in the places where apathy has made your faith a little too flabby, then just like that gym membership, daring calls for a commitment if you want any sort of reward. When you dare to step out, to put a dream into action, to conquer a new mountain, you are signing up to make an investment of time and energy to see those things happen in your life. Daring requires discipline, and that discipline needs to be consistent if it is going to overwhelm all the places where it may face resistance.

The decision to dare to step out is a great starting point, but it can also become a premature finishing line. We can sign up for the adventure only to change our mind when we see the adverse weather. Motivation only lasts for so long, and the door that opened for us can just as easily be closed through our neglect. If we are not deliberate about living a life of daring, then we will find—just like with my gym membership—the commitment to dare has become a one-time investment with a one-off return. After a while we stop showing up for the workout that we know daring demands, and instead choose to slip back into a preference for comfort over change.

Where not visiting the gym physically will mean we become less fit and agile, the consequences of being undisciplined in our daring go much deeper spiritually. As we remove the hunger and passion to keep daring, we allow apathy and passivity to take their place. Without the challenge we remain unchanged and lose our spiritual flexibility. We become more rigid in our ways and less open to being clay in the Potter's hand.

Without the

challenge we remain

unchanged.

THE POTTER AND THE CLAY

I went down to the potter's house, and I saw him working at the wheel. But the pot he was shaping from the clay was marred in his hands; so the potter formed it into another pot, shaping it as seemed best to him (Jeremiah 18:3-4).

We are the clay, and when the Potter asks us to dare to allow Him to mold and stretch our lives, our job is to stay pliable. When we say no to the journey of daring, we say no to the Potter who is molding us. We say, "I've reached my capacity," and we doubt the Potter's ability to continue His work.

I want to keep daring because I want to know that my life is constantly being molded. I want God's hands on my life, and the best way I know to ensure that happens is to stay pliable and be willing to let the wheel keep turning so God's vessel can continue to form.

As our ministry grew, Nat and I felt we had stretched spiritually in our daring to be. In so many ways we were on the Potter's wheel; we felt the kneading of the Holy Spirit, the molding of the Father's hands. And we discovered that the more we stayed in the process, the more we could see progress. We sensed that within the initial dare we took were many more dares waiting to be taken. It was like we had taken our first steps in this story, but now we needed to keep walking, sometimes running—even jumping. The daring had moved from being about an event to being about an ongoing commitment. We had said yes to our daring membership, and we were now each other's accountability partners so we would keep showing up and working out.

When I first signed up for the gym, the person who filled out the forms with me suggested I get a friend to sign up with me. They even offered me a discount if I could find another candidate for their membership. The reason they were so keen for me to bring a friend (apart from more membership fees for their gym, of course) was that they believed I was far more likely to stick with the program if I had someone doing it with me.

I have thought about that often while writing this book. I can recall so many instances on the Dare to Be journey when I felt like quitting, and the only reason I didn't walk away was the woman with whom I was walking. God knew this dare needed to be taken by both Nat and me. He provided a friend for the workout, a partner to keep us showing up on the days when we just wanted to stay in bed. He knew that attending the gym of daring would often require some extra accountability, and Nat and I can honestly say, looking back over our story, that that's exactly what we have found in each other.

In the moments when we have felt most weary, when we have wondered if we really wanted to keep going, one of us has stepped up and spoken up, assuring the other, "It's okay—you take a rest while I take the night watch."

Perhaps you don't want to dare alongside others because you would rather shape your own story than allow your life to be molded. You have become so used to being the boss that you don't want God, or another person God sends, to start suggesting something different from what you have already determined. But you need to allow God to mold you because even your best idea is nowhere near as great as the vessel God sees. When you stay on the Potter's wheel, you invite God to shape you—and others to see you being shaped.

Vulnerability is a dare many of us don't want to take, and yet if we really want to dare to be, it's a part of the membership that we can't opt out of. I remember one particularly hard day when Nat and I were on tour. We had an intense schedule with lots of back-to-back event dates. There were so many events, in fact, that Nat's voice was struggling, and we had to have a doctor join us on the bus. I had been away from home for a long time, and my kids wanted their mamma back. I was at the point where the ugly tears were about to make an appearance; I felt so vulnerable as I sat there on the bus.

I was ready to tear up my daring membership. I hadn't spoken to anyone about how low I was feeling…but that's when my accountability buddy came up behind me and said, "Hey, I wrote this new song, and I just feel like I should play it for you right now."

I was fixing my hair for that night's event, but Nat took the brush out of my hand and took over the hairdressing duty as I listened to the song. That's when my shoulders started shaking and those silent tears started falling. Nat knew I was hurting, and she didn't judge me for those feelings. In that moment, she knew the best way to help was just to be there and lift some of the weight. As the words of the song spoke to my internal storm, Nat prayed over me, and I felt a sense of relief as my perspective shifted. I was being molded. I didn't need to harden my heart; I needed to stay on the wheel.

It was in that same moment that I asked God for something very specific. I asked if He would give us daughters at the altar call that night. I prayed, *God, if I am leaving my son and daughter in order to be here, let it be so someone else's daughter can come home.* I needed to remember why I was there in the first place. I needed to dare again. If I was on that bus for some kind of superficial purpose, then this workout was way too costly. But if this dare was about someone's eternity, well, *Show me the weights and let's go!*

That night as I got to the altar call, I didn't want to open my eyes. But Nat nudged me and said, "Look." At the altar were so many women with their teenage daughters; the mothers had walked with them to the front, as these girls wanted to dare to begin a life with God at the center. That was the why behind the dare; it was the reason we were there.

FALTERING LIPS

When God dared Moses to deliver the children of Israel, Moses basically replied, "I can't do that; I can't speak." Moses saw his vulnerability and was closed off to the possibility of being used by God. But God knew that on the other side of this dare were thousands of people who needed to find freedom. He gave Moses his brother, Aaron, who became his daring accountability friend. Whenever Moses might say, "I can't show up and work out this calling today; I don't feel like I can even speak," Aaron would be able to reply, "I will help you speak."

> Moses said to the LORD, "Since I speak with faltering lips, why would Pharaoh listen to me?"
>
> Then the LORD said to Moses, "See, I have made you like God to Pharaoh, and your brother Aaron will be your prophet. You are to say everything I command you, and your brother Aaron is to tell Pharaoh to let the Israelites go out of his country" (Exodus 6:30–7:2).

Aaron came alongside Moses in many dares, whether it was addressing Pharaoh or defeating an army. Many knew Moses as the one God used to part the sea. Aaron, however, knew the Moses who was too weak to keep his arms extended so Joshua could defeat the Amalekites in battle.

> When Moses' hands grew tired, they took a stone and put it under him and he sat on it. Aaron and Hur held his hands up—one on one side, one on the other—so that his hands remained steady till sunset. So Joshua overcame the Amalekite army with the sword (Exodus 17:12-13).

Aaron knew that being his brother's "gym buddy" meant that on some days, the best thing he could do was just hold up his brother's arms. The dare they had taken was not for their own vanity but for saving thousands of people. Perhaps that's the greatest lesson we must learn on this journey of daring—the lesson that, in all our endeavors, God has a much greater agenda. If our daring is about attaining an accolade, a moment of fame, or some temporary prize, then we will eventually lose our momentum. The world needs fewer shooting stars and more guiding lights.

Daring to be is a journey for life. It's the adventure that has endless chapters, and that's a discovery Nat and I are continually making. When we first met and dared to start building Dare to Be as an event, we thought our act of obedience was complete—but we discovered that it was actually the start of a journey without a completion date.

THE MARATHON OF DARING

I remember years ago someone telling me that in ministry I should maximize the current moment, because it was likely to be gone as fast as it came. I was confused; they seemed to be suggesting I had one shot to do something, a small window in which to make my voice heard. I felt pressured by this advice, and so I took it to God. He spoke to me about two ways to do life: either treat life like a one-time sprint or treat it like a marathon. I am a runner, so this analogy made sense to me. Training for those two disciplines is very different; where the sprinter is more concerned with maximum speed, the marathon runner is concerned with a sustainable pace.

If you view the daring adventure as a sprint, you will go for it once, speak up once, start something new once, make a difference once. But if you see this

The world needs

fewer shooting stars

and more

guiding lights.

journey as a marathon, you will find a pace that allows you to keep daring, to go another mile, to run another hill. When that person told me I needed to sprint, I went away and decided I would rather be known not for a one-off *wow* moment but for a lifetime of service.

When Jesus invited the disciples to follow Him, it wasn't a dare to join Him on a one-time adventure. He dared them to follow Him for the rest of their lives. He didn't say, "I dare you to be part of one miracle." He dared them to *become* the miracle by bringing hope, kindness, truth, and deliverance to others.

Daring should be part of our daily discipline. If you still have breath in your lungs, then God still has a dare for you. Daring is for every age and stage of life; it's what keeps us spiritually agile and alert to our destiny. We as the righteous are called to be bold and advance the kingdom, to be salt and light, to be difference makers and hope bringers. That means we all have to keep daring to be. When we stop daring, we start stagnating—and that's why we must dare to dare again.

Moses didn't just dare to speak to Pharaoh through Aaron. He dared to stretch his hand over the waters before they parted, to find the wisdom to lead the way for many in the wilderness. Moses had to dare on a daily basis.

Joshua had to dare to share a good report in the face of negativity, to believe when nearly everyone else was filled with unbelief. Then he had to dare to take a city in a seemingly illogical way. He had to dare to lead when he likely felt unqualified and scared. He had to keep daring so he could possess the inheritance he believed was promised to him.

We can use our fallen lives as an excuse to give up daring. Yet consider David, who had to dare to humble himself after his sin with Bathsheba. It was David's humility that opened the way for him to get up and carry on in his calling as king. And it was the humbling of a proud Pharisee named Saul that made the way for the ministry of the apostle Paul. It was the humbling of a proud commander named Naaman that opened the pathway to healing.

We can also use our stage of life as a reason to stop daring. We think, *Well, I dared to do great things for You when I was young, Lord, but now I am old. I guess my daring days are over.* As if God were unable to use our latter years as well as our earlier ones! Consider Sarah, who had to dare to hope again and become a mother in her nineties. We need those who have journeyed longer to keep teaching us how to dare to be. We need the example of Caleb, who the Bible says was a man of a different spirit. He had a spirit that wouldn't let go, full of tenacity and bravery; he committed to keep daring until he saw all he knew he was destined to see.

> Just as the LORD promised, he has kept me alive for forty-five years since the time he said this to Moses, while Israel moved about in the wilderness. So here I am today, eighty-five years old! I am still as strong today as the day Moses sent me out; I'm just as vigorous to go out to battle now as I was then. Now give me this hill country that the LORD promised me that day. You yourself heard then that the Anakites were there and their cities were large and fortified, but, the LORD helping me, I will drive them out just as he said (Joshua 14:10-12).

What land do you need to dare again to take? What child do you need to dare again to believe for? What breakthrough do you need to dare again to attain? Perhaps you dared to believe God for provision when you found yourself in a time of need, but now that you find yourself with resources, you have quit daring to be generous. What if God wants you to dare not just for your need but for the seed to give more and bless more? What if the first step of your daring was about stretching your faith, and the next dare is about stretching your faithfulness?

Perhaps you dared at one point to believe God for that job which you now have, but what if you dared to go for that promotion, to step up more in your workplace? What if you dared to move to the new city? What if you dared to apply to the college or program that intimidates you? What if you dared to reconcile with an estranged friend or family member? What if you dared to forgive a legitimate wrong? What if you dared to reach out to someone who's hurting in the pew beside you? What if you dared to open your home and offer hospitality?

Don't allow comfort to cause you to compromise. Instead, keep daring to be all God has called you to be.

Nat and I have faced this challenge on a regular basis. We dared to say yes to the friendship, and that led to us daring to be in ministry together—and the dares just kept coming. There was the dare to start the Dare to Be Foundation, then the dare to write our first devotional and the dare to start a Bible curriculum. Every time we embarked upon a dare, it led to another one. It was like our *yes* was the engine that got the train moving, and the train cars just kept being added on; with each new dare we accepted, we were helping more passengers.

When we talked about starting a podcast, we were a little embarrassed to admit that neither of us really knew that much about them. We were hesitant to say yes to something we felt wasn't a fit for us. We talked with the people who had approached us with the idea, and they suggested we just give it a try, so we agreed to go into the studio. We were aware of the time and expense this was incurring as we booked the facility and hired the people to make it happen.

As we sat across the table for our first recording, we looked at each other and said our much-loved and often-used phrase, "Yay for me, I'm daring to be!" It was our way of saying to each other, "Here we go again—let's hope this works out." About 30 minutes into the recording, we suddenly found this flow; our conversation felt so easy even though the format was unfamiliar. We recorded something that, had we refused to take the dare, would never have come into existence. As I write this, we have just agreed to our second season of the Dare to Be podcast. When I think about the thousands who have listened in on these conversations, I am reminded again that the dare is always about so much more than we can ever realize in the moment of acceptance.

We started this book with "once upon a time," so it seems appropriate to ask, "What's the happily ever after?" For Nat and me, it's the woman who was lost but has been found. It's the heroine who helped everyone else and whom we got to help and honor. It's the teenager who was searching for something and found strength for her story. It's the heart that was healed, the marriage that was restored, the light that shone into someone's darkness. The dare is about all those happily ever afters and more.

Friend, we are all indebted in some way to someone's willingness to dare and dare again. Perhaps for you it was a praying parent or a witnessing colleague, the generous stranger or the faithful friend. It was the daring of heaven that became the salvation of earth. It was the daring of a Savior that secured our happily ever after.

When we make the story about us, we miss the beauty of an ending that becomes so much more than any one of us. We are not writing a personal fairy tale; we are writing our chapter in history. We are adding our page to the pages of those who dared before us. We are the ones right now with the responsibility to dare to be all God says we can be, to dare to be all our world needs to see, to dare to be again and again and again.

This story is far from over. In fact, it's only getting started. Whatever chapter of your life you find yourself in, my friend, we are praying you would take courage, pick up the pen, and dare to be all over again.

Don't allow

comfort to cause you

to compromise.

NOTES FROM NATALIE

As we've been writing this book, looking back at our Dare to Be moments, we can see again and again how our responsibility has been to respond in obedience to God's faithfulness. Our commitment has been to dare to believe that God is who He says He is, that we can take Him at His word. What we may not see today or even tomorrow, we can have confidence we will see in the end. We will see that God was faithful all along, just as we are promised in Scripture.

> I remain confident of this:
>> I will see the goodness of the LORD
>> in the land of the living (Psalm 27:13).

Over the years, a song has been playing in my head. It's one I began to sing long before we launched Dare to Be. One night, in that pivotal year I shared with you back at the beginning of this book, I had the privilege of performing "Bring It All Together" with Wynonna Judd at the Ryman Auditorium in Nashville. Just minutes before I got to sing on that world-famous stage, my phone rang. It was the specialist who had been working with me and my husband, and he confirmed the news that I had been dreading. There was less than a 3 percent chance that we would ever conceive naturally.

"Bring It All Together" is based on Romans 8:28, which reminds us that God works all things together for the good of those who love Him. That night, despite the words I was singing, I did not feel like celebrating God's faithfulness. Yet over the years, this truth has become my confession. I have had to believe He is always true—not just sometimes, but *always*. Even when the dream has seemed preposterous, even when I thought I would never laugh again, even when I couldn't see a path, I have had to confess that God would bring it all together for good.

This is the same in every dream we imagine, every adventure we set out on, every dare we take. In the struggle, in the vulnerability, in the weariness, our confession does not have to match our emotions. I spend a lot of time in the book of Psalms, and I think the reason is because the psalms were written by people who were on an emotional roller coaster, just like me. One day I can feel abandoned and alone, and I read,

> Look and see, there is no one at my right hand;
>   no one is concerned for me.
> I have no refuge;
>   no one cares for my life (Psalm 142:4).

The next day I can feel surrounded by the goodness of God, and I read,

> You make me glad by your deeds, LORD;
> I sing for joy at what your hands have done (Psalm 92:4).

When we face heartbreak, failure, or disappointments, we tend to ask questions of God. Charl and I have been honest with you about our Dare to Be journey in this book. We did not and do not have it all together all the time. But when we confess the goodness of God over our lives, even when we struggle to believe it, that's when the breakthrough comes. It's when we realize once again that it's all about who He is, regardless of whether our plans turn out the way we dream they will.

So as we close this book together, we dare you to dare again. Do it now. Sing and shout your praise wherever you are. Step out with obedience into God's faithfulness as, like us, you dare to follow the Master's plan.

I know there will come a day of healing
We will see the master plan
We will celebrate His faithfulness
And we'll sing and we'll shout
Praise His name

He's gonna take your pain
He's gonna take your doubt
He's gonna bring it all together
Bring it all together
Gonna make you happy
He's gonna make you laugh out loud
He's gonna bring it all together
Bring it all together for good [10]

QUESTIONS FOR DISCUSSION AND REFLECTION

- What will your next steps of daring be?

- What can you do today to start the change for tomorrow?

- What personal dares do you need to take? Make a list, commit it to God, and *dare to be*.

THE PRAYER THAT DARES

Lord, You are able, and You are faithful.
Lord, You are all-powerful and all-knowing.
Teach my heart how to dare to be all You have called me to be.
Let my life become the unfolding story that You have planned for me.
Let my fears be silenced and my faith amplified,
for I know You have planned good things for my life.
All that concerns me You have already covered with Your grace and mercy,
so I dare to believe in who You say I am.
I dare to begin the work for Your greater plan.
I dare to trust You with what I see and what I can't yet perceive.
Lord, thank You for choosing me.
Thank You for going before me.
Thank You for setting a table in the presence of my enemies.
I dare to declare my greatest days are ahead.
I dare to build a life that is overflowing with Your life.
I dare to believe I was born for such a time as this.
Lord, I dare to pick up the pen and write again.
Lord, let my story bring You all the glory.
Amen.

SONG LYRIC CREDITS

DARE TO BE...ONCE UPON A TIME

1. "Awaken"

   Words and music by Natalie Grant, Robert Graves, Jason McArthur, and Joy Williams

   © 2005 New Spring Publishing, Inc./Mge Songs/Bridge Building Music/Logansong Music (All adm. by CapitolCMGPublishing.com) Songs of Razor and Tie (All rights for Songs of Razor and Tie administered by Concord Music Publishing) All rights reserved. Used by permission.

   Reprinted by permission of Hal Leonard LLC.

DARE TO BELIEVE

2. "Do It Through Me"

   Words and music by Natalie Grant, Bernie Herms, and Paul Duncan

   © 2020 NG Entertainment (admin. by Music Services) Centricity Music Publishing (Adm at CapitolCMGPublishing.com) Sony Music Publishing (US) LLC, Pure Note Publishing Worldwide. All rights obo Sony Music Publishing (US) LLC and Pure Note Publishing Worldwide administered by Sony Music Publishing (US) LLC, 424 Church Street Suite 1200, Nashville Tennessee 37219. All rights reserved. Used by permission.

DARE TO BE REAL

3. "The Real Me"

   Words and music by Natalie Grant

   © Songs of Razor and Tie (All rights for Songs of Razor and Tie administered by Concord Music Publishing) All rights reserved. Used by permission.

   Reprinted by permission of Hal Leonard LLC.

DARE TO PAUSE

4. "Face To Face"

   Words and music by Bernie Herms, Natalie Grant, and Paul Duncan

   © 2020 Centricity Music Publishing (Adm. by CapitolCMGPublishing.com) NG Entertainment (Adm. by Music Services) Sony Music Publishing (US) LLC, Pure Note Publishing Worldwide (All rights obo Sony Music Publishing (US) LLC and Pure Note Publishing Worldwide administered by Sony Music Publishing (US) LLC, 424 Church Street Suite 1200, Nashville Tennessee 37219). All rights reserved. Used by permission.

DARE TO BEGIN

5. "Hurricane"

Words and music by Cindy Morgan, Natalie Grant, and Matt Bronleewe

© 2013 Green Bike Music/Simple Tense Songs/SeeSeeBubba Songs (Adm. by Music Services) So Essential Tunes/Forest for the Trees Music (Adm. by EssentialMusicPublishing.com) All rights reserved. Used by permission.

DARE TO BUILD

6. "My Weapon"

Words and music by Ryan Ellis, Natalie Grant, Andrew Bergthold, Benji Cowart, and Jonathan Jay

© 2020 All Essential Music/Ryan Ellis Publishing Designee (Adm. by EssentialMusicPublishing.com) Heritage Worship Music Publishing/Let There Be Songs (Adm. by Heritage Worship Music Publishing)/Maverick City Publishing (Adm. by Heritage Worship Music Publishing) Curb Songs/West Coast Worship/Goodbye 99 (Adm. by Curb Songs) All rights reserved. Used by permission.

DARE TO FAIL

7. "Who Else"

Words and music by Sam Mizell, Natalie Grant, and Becca Mizell

© 2020 NG Entertainment (Adm. By Music Services) Shepherd and Marble Music/Underneath the Willowtree Music (Both adm. by CMG Worldwide, Inc.) All rights reserved. Used by permission.

DARE TO SHARE

8. "No Stranger"

Words and music by Bernie Herms, Natalie Grant, and Paul Duncan

2020 Centricity Music Publishing (Adm. by CapitolCMGPublishing.com) NG Entertainment (Adm. by Music Services) Sony Music Publishing (US) LLC, Pure Note Publishing Worldwide (All rights obo Sony Music Publishing (US) LLC and Pure Note Publishing Worldwide administered by Sony Music Publishing (US) LLC, 424 Church Street Suite 1200, Nashville Tennessee 37219). All rights reserved. Used by permission.

DARE TO TRUST

9. "King of the World"

Words and music by Natalie Grant, Sam Mizell, and Becca Mizell

© 2015 SeeSeeBubba Songs (Adm. by Music Services) BMG Platinum Songs/Takin' It To The Maxx (Adm. by BMG Rights Management (US) LLC/Maxx Melodies. All rights reserved. Used by permission.

DARE TO DARE AGAIN

10. "Bring It All Together"

Words and music by Shaun Shankel and Christa Wells

© 2005 Weimarhymes Publishing, Inc./ Cinco Ninos Publishing (Both adm. by Curb Songs) Shankel Songs. All rights reserved. Used by permission.

With more than 25 years in church leadership, **Charlotte Gambill** has committed her life to teaching, training, and investing in others. Both locally and globally, she has become a sought-after speaker and teacher. She is the founder of Cherish women's conference, a global gathering of women, and has launched We Are One and the Cherish foundation, initiatives bringing the power of kindness into the most broken of places. She is the author of 14 books, cofounder of the Dare To Be movement, and teaching pastor at Church of the Highlands, USA. Happily married for more than 25 years, she and her husband, Steve, lead Life Church with five campuses across Europe. They have two teenage children, Hope Cherish and Noah Brave.

As an eight-time GRAMMY® nominee and five-time GMA Dove Awards Female Vocalist of the Year, **Natalie Grant** has become an icon in Christian and gospel music. In addition to garnering more than 500 million streams and multiple number-one albums and singles on the Billboard charts, she is also a respected author and philanthropist. She is the cofounder of Hope for Justice, a nonprofit organization in the fight against human trafficking, which has 32 offices across 9 countries and 5 continents and helped 102,803 children in the last year.

To learn more about Harvest House books and
to read sample chapters, visit our website:

www.harvesthousepublishers.com

HARVEST HOUSE PUBLISHERS
EUGENE, OREGON